Looking for Eden

The Solo Albums *of* Ian Anderson

Richard Taylor

Looking for Eden

The Solo Albums of Ian Anderson

Richard Taylor

WYMER PUBLISHING
Bedford, England

First published in Great Britain in 2025
by Wymer Publishing
www.wymerpublishing.co.uk
Tel: 01234 326691
Wymer Publishing is a trading name of Wymer (UK) Ltd

© 2025 Wymer Publishing.

ISBN: 978-1-915246-75-2
(also available in eBook)

Edited by Laura Shenton

The Author hereby asserts his rights to be identified
as the author of this work in accordance with sections
77 to 78 of the Copyright, Designs & Patents Act 1988.

All rights reserved. No part of this publication may be
reproduced or transmitted in any form or by any means,
electronic or mechanical, including photocopying, or any
information storage and retrieval system, without written
permission from the publisher.

This publication is sold subject to the condition that it shall not,
by way of trade or otherwise, be lent, re-sold, hired out or
otherwise circulated without the publishers prior consent in any
form of binding or cover other than that in which it is published
and without a similar condition including this condition
being imposed on the subsequent purchaser.

Every effort has been made to trace the copyright holders of the
photographs in this book but some were unreachable. We would
be grateful if the photographers concerned would contact us.

Typeset by Andy Bishop / Tusseheia Creative
Printed by CMP, Dorset, England.

A catalogue record for this book is available from the British Library.

Cover design: Tusseheia Creative
Illustrations: Bekah Elliott

Contents

A Brief Introduction   9
The Solo Artist   11
Ranking the Albums   17
The Illustrations   19

Chapter 1 Walk Into Light   23
Chapter 2 Divinities: Twelve Dances With God   41
Chapter 3 The Secret Language Of Birds   63
Chapter 4 Rupi's Dance   85
Chapter 5 TAAB 2 (Thick As A Brick 2)   103
Chapter 6 Homo Erraticus   123

Conclusion   143
Acknowledgements   152
Bibliography   153
About The Author   155

A Brief Introduction

On Ian Anderson's debut solo album *Walk Into Light* (1983), there is a song on side two of the vinyl called "Looking For Eden." Despite the perhaps overcooked electronic sound typical of the entire album, this track remains a personal favourite of mine, both for its lyrical sentiment and its music. You can read more about the song in Chapter 1 but suffice it to say that I've borrowed its title for this book.

I suspect that throughout his solo career, Ian Anderson has been searching for his own musical Eden — a pursuit that, in certain exceptional songs, he comes remarkably close to achieving, if not entirely realising. For the rest of us mere mortals, the quest to find our ideal geographical or spiritual sanctuary — whether we call it Eden, Utopia, or Nirvana — is an intrinsic part of the human condition. Perhaps if Ian had written a song titled "Looking for Tescos," it wouldn't have quite resonated in the same way and would not have cut the mustard as a title!

Interestingly, there's a nice bit of symmetry in the final song on his most recent solo album, *Homo Erraticus* (2014). "Cold Dead Reckoning" hints at a future Eden — a "future garden of earthly delight to come" —projected in our near future (2044). This makes "Looking for Eden" a title I'm entirely content to live with and strive for. Let's hope Ian's vision of a new Eden becomes a reality, but...

The book begins with a discussion of Ian Anderson as a solo artist, followed by an explanation of how I will rank the albums to determine which one I believe is the best. Of course, it's entirely expected — and perfectly valid — that you may disagree with my objectively subjective choice.

As is my habit (a trait, I confess, of my former life as a "ten out of ten" teacher), I do enjoy incorporating some scoring action to see which songs — and, more importantly, which album —

emerge as my favourites. At this stage, before revisiting all six albums after so many years, I genuinely don't know which one will come out on top.

The main body of the book comprises six major chapters, each offering a song-by-song analysis of one of the albums. In the Conclusion, I will reveal my final rankings of the albums and my favourite songs — but not before! So, no sneaky peeking, or I'll have to confiscate the book.

Throughout the book, I use the terms "song" and "track" interchangeably. Generally, I refer to "song" when discussing lyrics and "track" when focusing on the music itself.

To the best of my knowledge, no one has written a dedicated book on Ian Anderson's solo albums before. They've typically only been mentioned in passing within books and magazines about Jethro Tull, so this might well qualify as a "first edition" on the subject.

Right then — time to dig out some dusty vinyl, a few frayed cassette tapes, and the odd CD of the six albums.

Here we go. Wish me "good luck"!

The Solo Artist

The history of rock music is filled with notable bandleaders or key members who have ventured into solo careers. For some, this involves a permanent departure from the band, such as Peter Gabriel leaving Genesis or Roger Waters parting ways with Pink Floyd. For others, their solo work runs (more or less) concurrently with the continuation of the band's activities, with the artist eventually returning to the fold. It is this second category that applies to Ian Anderson and Jethro Tull.

On the whole, I suspect that this kind of solo detour, followed by a return to the band, has not often been a significant commercial success—though there is one remarkable exception. That said, commercial success isn't always the goal. For many artists, including Ian Anderson, artistic integrity is the driving force.

In this book, I intend to argue that Ian Anderson's solo albums are a wonderful collection of hidden gems. They are well worth listening to and discussing, even though they didn't achieve strong sales. After all, Ian is not the only famous rock star to encounter a few retail challenges when striking out on his own!

The Rolling Stones have produced 31 studio albums, while Mick Jagger has released five solo albums, mainly during the 1980s when he and Keith Richards were "not speaking." The Stones have sold 200 million albums, whereas Mick's solo efforts only managed 3 million—a mere 1.5% of the band's sales.

For Freddie Mercury, the comparison is even more stark. Queen recorded 15 studio albums with a staggering 300 million sales, while Freddie's two solo albums sold a combined total of just 1 million. This gives Freddie a solo sales percentage of only 0.33%.

In contrast, Phil Collins presents a rare exception. In the early 1970s, he was primarily known as a highly skilled prog-rock drummer in Genesis, providing harmonies alongside

Peter Gabriel. However, his 1980 debut solo album, *Face Value*, prompted by his marriage breakdown, sold zillions and after that he never looked back in anger. Phil went on to release eight solo studio albums, compared to Genesis's 15, yet remarkably sold 150 million albums as a solo artist and an equal 150 million with Genesis. By my calculations, this gives Phil a sales percentage of 100% — a feat few can match.

Phil did well and his success is exceptional, but it underscores how uncommon it is for solo ventures to rival or surpass the parent group. I suspect Freddie wouldn't "give a fig, darling" about his sales comparison today, while Mick — ever the competitor — might feel slightly irked by his modest solo numbers. Like Ian Anderson, both Mick and Freddie eventually returned to their respective bands after their solo interludes. Phil, on the other hand, moved fluidly between his solo career and his work with Genesis, with the latter undoubtedly benefiting from his immense popularity.

So, where does this leave Ian Anderson and Jethro Tull? The band has released 24 studio albums (and counting), while Ian, as a solo artist, has produced six. By early 2024, Jethro Tull had performed 3,207 gigs, compared to Ian's 1,038 solo performances. This means that roughly a quarter to a third of Ian's working life has been dedicated to his solo career.

It is widely recognised within the Jethro Tull universe that the band has sold over 60 million albums. However, determining — or even "guestimating" — Ian's solo album sales is trickier. My best calculation suggests sales of up to a million across his six albums, giving Ian a solo percentage of 1.6%. This figure puts him ahead of Freddie Mercury and fractionally ahead of Mick Jagger but leaves him trailing, unsurprisingly, behind the ubiquitous Phil Collins (as almost everyone else does).

While these statistics are a bit of light-hearted fun, I would argue that Ian's solo work holds significant artistic credibility. His solo albums were essential to his growth as a writer and performer and made valuable contributions to the concurrent and future output of Jethro Tull. In my humble opinion, all six solo albums are of a high standard, varied (much like Tull albums), enjoyable to listen to, and well worth analysing and discussing. Being the fan that I am, I genuinely prefer listening to Ian's solo work over that of Mick Jagger, Freddie Mercury, or — even, dare I say it — Phil Collins. (But that's our little secret. Don't tell Phil!)

So, what is it about solo albums and rock stars? There may be several reasons why artists feel compelled to go it alone, even though the odds are they'll lose money — unless, of course, they're Uncle Phil. Some possible motivations for embarking on a solo venture might include:

1) Too many songs and too little album space.

This particular reason wouldn't have applied to Ian Anderson in the late 1960s and 1970s. During that time, he was able to include all the songs he wanted on Jethro Tull albums, which were released annually, and he was the band's sole writer (aside from J.S. Bach, whose "Bourée" was an exception, and being long deceased, was unlikely to claim any more album slots). Between 1968 and 1980, Tull produced 13 albums, each roughly 40 minutes long — almost nine hours of Anderson's music — meaning there was little need for additional album space.

A prime example of a solo album born from a writer's frustration at not being able to release their material is George Harrison's triple album *All Things Must Pass* (1970). Harrison, competing for space on Beatles albums alongside Lennon and McCartney — two of the greatest songwriters of all time — had amassed a substantial backlog of songs, waiting to showcase his own brilliance.

One of the great "what if" moments in music history is speculating about what might have featured on the next Beatles album if they hadn't split in 1970. Tracks like "Instant Karma" (John), "Another Day" (Paul), "It Don't Come Easy" (Ringo), and the iconic "My Sweet Lord" (George) could have formed the core of a truly spectacular record. Even so, Harrison — "The Quiet One" — would likely still have needed a double solo album to release other magnificent tracks such as "Wah Wah," "All Things Must Pass," and "What Is Life," even if the Fab Four had stayed together.

2) Falling out.

Ian Anderson never experienced the kind of musical or personal falling out that would compel him to work alone, away from Jethro Tull. There was no dramatic moment of pique or conflict; artistically, he simply wanted to explore something different.

A prime example of a split leading to a solo career, however, is Roger Waters' departure from — or attempted shutdown of — Pink Floyd. Waters fell out with his bandmates, particularly Dave Gilmour, both musically and personally. When Pink Floyd reformed in 1989 without him, they "left" Waters, making him somewhat agitated and he found himself in significant legal conflict with the band.

3) A different musical approach.

This point certainly applies to Ian Anderson, particularly with his first two solo albums. *Walk Into Light* was an "electronica à la Thomas Dolby" album, while *Divinities: Twelve Dances With God* was a classical album. There was absolutely no way to infinity and beyond could these have been released as Jethro Tull albums — they were simply too far removed from the band's style.

With subsequent solo records, Ian's approach became more akin to Tull's, especially with *Thick As A Brick 2* (*TAAB2*) and *Homo Erraticus*, which were overtly prog rock, concept album, Tull-like in style and substance.

That said, many solo albums by other artists often sound like extensions of their parent band, where the rock star in question writes band-style songs but uses predominantly acoustic instruments. This was true of Ian's middle two solo releases, *The Secret Language Of Birds* and *Rupi's Dance*. These albums were very much in the spirit of Tull, or "Tull-lite," with only the occasional hint of electric guitar.

4) Request from the record company.

This is particularly relevant to *Divinities* as Ian has often stated that he was approached to create the album by the classical division of EMI. The company likely believed that a rock/classical crossover would generate pots of money. It didn't!

5) More personal control

As the main creative force in Jethro Tull, Ian Anderson could always do as he pleased with the band's albums, although perhaps he couldn't emphasise his own name above the others, given that Tull operated as a "democratic group." By the time of his last two solo albums in the 2010s, after Tull's split in 2011, it seemed clear that Ian wanted to make it even more apparent that he was solely in the driving seat. *Thick As A Brick 2* and *Homo Erraticus* were unmistakably "Tull heavy," but they were very much written and arranged by Ian Anderson alone, with little doubt about who was behind their creation and creativity.

***

It's time to mention the strange and rather sad tale of the first "solo" album... that never truly was. While it eventually emerged as a Jethro Tull album, it retained its "solo" moniker as *A* — for Anderson — and the full story is covered in detail in various books about Jethro Tull, including my own *Life Is A Long Song*.

In 1979, the band was struck by the tragic death of bassist John Glascock. After the *Stormwatch* tour in early 1980, it was agreed that Jethro Tull would take a break. However, Ian Anderson was eager to continue working musically with Eddie Jobson, whom he had met when his band, UK, supported Tull. This led to the idea of a solo album. Eddie brought along his drummer friend Mark Craney, and Ian enlisted new Tull bassist Dave Pegg to contribute. But something was still missing — so in stepped Martin Barre, adding his signature power chords, riffs, and shredding to the mix.

At this point, the record company intervened, insisting that it had to be a Jethro Tull album. As a result, John Evan, David Palmer, and Barrie Barlow were left out, as they hadn't played on the record. They were then informed by fax that they were no longer required for future Tull projects. It was a sad chapter in Tull's history, but for the purposes of this book, it represents a fascinating "what if" moment.

Had Ian, with the support of just Eddie Jobson, gone ahead and released *A* as a solo album, *Walk Into Light* (1983), with

Peter-John Vettese, might never have happened. The band's break-up of the 1970s line up could have been avoided, and I might not be writing this book. In reality, though, *A*, the Tull album, was a near miss as Ian's first solo album.

As I mentioned earlier, I am extremely fond of all of Ian's solo work. Some of it is absolutely outstanding, and I'm very much looking forward to undertaking an album-by-album, track-by-track analysis of the eighty-two wonderful songs and instrumentals that Ian Anderson has offered across his six solo albums.

Although *The Zealot Gene* by Jethro Tull was released in 2022, Ian Anderson had been planning it as a Tull album since 2017. He recognised that using the Tull name might result in higher sales and, as he says, it was also a way to acknowledge the contributions of the more or less permanent Ian Anderson Band. Following *The Zealot Gene*, Tull also released *RökFlöte* in 2023, and *Curious Ruminant* in 2025.

Given the current trajectory, I think it's unlikely that Ian will release any more solo albums during the remainder of his recording career. However, if he does, I'll be forced to write a follow-up book or add an extra chapter — so, please, Ian, no more solo albums!

Ranking The Albums

In my *Life Is A Long Song* Jethro Tull book, I decided to rank the 33 songs I selected, purely for fun, to spark discussion among fans, readers, and nerdy types alike. I did this by awarding each song a score out of 10, based on factors like lyrics, melody, production, and, ultimately, how much I liked the track. It was very much a deliberately subjective exercise, no doubt designed to either please or perhaps infuriate you, the readers, but also to provide an entertaining discussion. After all, everyone loves a good ranking!

Now, I want to explain how I will rank the six albums in this book. It's been a long time since I last listened to them in detail — certainly not in the deep dive I'll be doing for this book. I have no idea which of the six albums will come out on top, and if I did, I certainly wouldn't tell you until the Conclusion.

For each album, I will score each song/track out of 20 (no half marks), then add up the scores and divide by the number of songs/tracks on the album to calculate an average score. This will give me an overall mark for each album. This process will also help me determine my ten favourite Ian Anderson tracks out of the eighty-two he has created, which I will reveal — surreptitiously and not now — at the end, in the Conclusion. This is intended to build anticipation and excitement for the final ranking and the crowning of the winning album, which will, of course, serve as a fitting end to the book.

Of course, you could add up and average the scores yourself before the Conclusion, or even sneak a peek, but where's the fun in that? Until then, my lips and pen are sealed. I will base my song ratings on factors like music, lyrics, production, and so on, but ultimately, they reflect my personal, subjective view of what I like. You are, of course, free to disagree with my ratings and choices — "definitely maybe" even! You could write your own scores in the margins if you like and calculate your own final rankings, but please make sure to get the book owner's permission first. You've been warned.

So, from "Fly By Night" (*Walk Into Light*) to "Cold Dead Reckoning" (*Homo Erraticus*), let's begin! I wish you all the best of luck and happiness with your own rankings!

The Illustrations

As with my earlier *Life Is A Long Song: A Compendium of Jethro Tull in 33 1/3 Songs* book, I was fortunate again to work with the very talented line drawing artist, Bekah Elliott. I decided, as well as a "Looking For Eden" front piece, I wanted to have bookend illustrations for each of the 6 solo album chapters, therefore making 13 illustrations in total.

I must point out that Bekah is not a particular fan of Ian Anderson, nor Jethro Tull and has not been over familiar with the music but I felt that could work to my advantage. In the last book, and this one, what I did not want were caricature cartoonist embellishments of Ian Anderson in particular, which you can find in other publications and on social media, which someone who was a Tull fan would have done. I wanted an illustrator with an uncluttered, non-IA and JT mindset, who would work from the album titles, a fresh with no hint of knowledgeable bias. I certainly got that from Bekah, as a non-fan, although there is a rumour she is rather partial to Opeth, who just might have been influenced by Ian and Jethro Tull a little bit, here and there, now and again.

Meanwhile, I wanted the illustrations to say something new, perhaps in an unexpected weird, enigmatic, yet entertaining way that would give pause for thought and maybe even provoke discussion. It has to be all done in the best prog rock art tradition of course with just a few clues down below, to help you on your ponderingly artistic journey of discovery.

The front piece represents "Looking For Eden," with the observer, peering into the garden, through the dark formidable gates, nearly there, but not quite. The leafy vines are there to show floral growth here and in all the illustrations, to give an Eden-esque backdrop.

"Walk Into Light" has the dreaded synthesiser in the (spot) light but luckily for all of us, it is heading for the exit at the end of the chapter.

It is an open and shut camera case for "Divinities: Twelve Dances With God." Violin heads and flute varieties complete the picture and the vines will not go away.

The Bird of Paradise for "The Secret Language Of Birds" likes an artist's pose and then on the way out, a winged display. It just could be an acoustic album, you can tell.

Rupi, the cat likes a tambourine and an accordion, when not getting tangled up in the vines. For "Rupi's Dance."

The perfect day for our favourite brick, with "Thick as A Brick 2." Up and coming with the Sun and down and leaving with the Moon

With "Home Erraticus", there are Ernist's, Gerald's and Ian's 8 chronicled possibilities. On the last illustration there is room in the petals, for you to write the answers. At this point both myself and Bekah would like to thank the vines, for their co-starring role, in all the illustrations.

Bekah says:

"I very much enjoyed doing the pictures but working out quite what Richard wanted was challenging but fun. Despite taking many long hard hours, I do enjoy monochromatic pen drawing by hand. The vines linking all the illustrations together, climbing through from Eden, came from me. I was pleased that Richard approved. Finally, I am still not really an Ian Anderson or Jethro Tull fan but things change, don't they?"

1
Walk Into Light

By 1983, Jethro Tull had welcomed a new whiz-kid keyboard player, Peter-John Vettese. Peter was an exceptional musicologist and an outstanding technocrat, particularly when it came to the early 1980s' world of synths, samplers, and drum machines. In other words, when he pressed the right musical keys, he also knew how to hit the right technical buttons, in the correct order, simultaneously. He was everything you could want in a top-notch, all-round 1983 musical polymath and virtuoso player. Additionally, he was — and still is — a brilliant arranger and interpreter of other people's music, which made him the perfect collaborator for Ian Anderson on his first solo album.

While *Divinities: Twelve Dances With God* from the nineties is a very different beast — a classical flute album — Ian again worked almost exclusively with another keyboard wizard, Andrew (or "Andy," as he was first known for Tull albums) Giddings. Interestingly, no one played guitar on that album. However, this would change over the course of Ian's six solo albums, with plenty of acoustic and electric guitar appearing by the time of *Homo Erraticus* in 2014. But I digress...

After *Broadsword And The Beast* and the subsequent tours, drummer Gerry Conway left the band. Tragically, Gerry passed away in 2024, and there is a tribute to him in the chapter on *The Secret Language Of Birds*, which he played on as a session musician. Ian, ever the prolific writer, still had a wealth of great songs to release and decided to go solo, incorporating the new keyboard and synthesiser sounds that were characteristic of the era. This also meant using a "diabolical" drum machine — more on that later.

Ironically, despite it being a solo album, Ian collaborated with Peter on five of the twelve tracks, co-writing with him. As the virtually exclusive writer for Jethro Tull, this was a departure for Ian, but one that was to continue on *Under Wraps*. Since then, however, it has been Ian writing almost exclusively, both with Tull and solo.

This shift was likely not what Ian originally planned, nor what fans expected, but Peter's substantial contributions are spread across the entire album and deserve recognition.

Most of the keyboard work is very much of its time, which in that context is entirely appropriate. Describing Peter's contribution is tricky, but let's say it was dynamically "sparkling." If anything, perhaps it sparkles a bit too much at times. There might have been room for more "gaps" in the keyboard parts, allowing the songs to breathe a little more. Of course, filling those spaces with more acoustic guitar and flute would have been an option — but where would the experimental fun have been in that?

There are two ways, I think, to approach *Walk Into Light* as an album. First, instrumentally, there was a noticeable lack of flute and guitar — elements one might expect from Ian Anderson. Instead, the album is dominated almost entirely by keyboards and drum machines, leading some critics (though not me) to describe it as having a "dry, cold" sound. It could be said to have a very mechanised, automated, non-acoustic feel, which, for many fans and reviewers, didn't quite work.

My own particular issue lies with the use of the Mr A Linn Drum, the robot drummer on *Walk Into Light* and Jethro Tull's *Under Wraps*. It just sounds... well, dreadful, with a capital D. Much like *Under Wraps*, the album would have greatly benefitted from the inclusion of a real drummer, something that could have made a world of difference. Come on, Ian, you know you want to! While there's a chance this might happen for *Under Wraps,* especially after some comments by Ian along these lines in interviews in February 2025, that there could be a new recording featuring a flesh and blood live drummer, it's not going to happen with *Walk Into Light*. That said, as an experiment and a step forward in his own musical development, it was a commendable effort.

Predictably, fans were expecting flute, acoustic guitar, and vocals, but instead they got synths, drum machines, and vocals. At least the singing voice remained consistent. Ian's vocal performance on this album is wonderfully understated — he's not straining as he does on *Under Wraps*, and this was before his mid-eighties throat problems. In 2025, his current vocal state might lend itself beautifully to some of these tracks, like "Fly By Night," with their more spoken, less forceful passages.

Secondly, what about the songs? There are some decent tracks, some good ones, and a few absolute gems that deserve a place on any Tull album — or even in the broader realm of classic rock — undiminished by the "electronica" sound. In my view, four of the tracks stand out as exceptional, including "Looking For Eden." With its beautiful melodic tune and poignant, searching lyrics, it could easily serve as a fitting title for this book and it does!

Walk Into Light was released on 18th November 1983 in the UK, with a slightly later release in the USA. It briefly reached No. 78 in the UK album charts, and that was about it — it was a non-starter and a commercial flop. The vinyl album sleeve features a full list of the keyboards and other equipment played by Ian and Peter, which reads like this: Rhodes Chroma and Expander, Yamaha CP80, Roland JP8, Promars, MC202, Emulator (with original user samples), and Ludwig drums via the Linn Drum Computer.

It sounds very impressive — high-tech, no doubt — but I do not have a clue of what most of it actually does, apart from perhaps the drumming tech bits. If you're curious for more details, I suggest you contact Peter-John Vettese at HiTecMusicalMomentsOfThe80s.com, but don't tell him I sent you.

That said, despite all this, it doesn't sound as bad instrumentally as one might expect. As mentioned earlier, the keyboard playing does "sparkle." Combined with Ian's more traditional contributions on electric and bass guitars, plus occasional flute trills for good measure, it's more than halfway decent most of the time. The one noticeable absence, however, is any sign of an acoustic guitar.

Fly By Night *(Anderson, Vettese)*

A "fly by night" refers to someone of dubious character who sneaks off under the cover of darkness to avoid financial or social responsibilities, or even family obligations. It could also describe a business — unreliable, untrustworthy, a "here today, gone tomorrow" venture that vanishes when no one is paying attention. Either way, a "fly by night" is someone who cannot be relied upon, someone you certainly wouldn't want to lend your Tull albums to.

However, Ian's "Fly By Night" seems to be a fairly conventional break-up song (I think it's safe to assume Ian wrote all the lyrics for the album). Initially, the songwriter seems intent on running off alone in the early hours, showing a certain irresponsibility. Yet, there's a hint of plaintive apology in the early verses. By the final verse, regret sets in, and it seems both parties are less than happy. There's an impression that both lovers now want to "fly by night" together, seeking a fresh start somewhere else... or at least, that's how I interpret it.

So, "let's fly" becomes an evocative invitation at the end of the song, allowing the instrumental section to soar off into the nighttime ether, where the lovers may well live happily ever after... perhaps. As I've mentioned before, I do find Ian's lyrics tricky at times — though you may well have a different interpretation and disagree.

Compared to the length of the song, the lyrics are relatively sparse, but I think they are wonderfully delivered by Ian — understated yet full of warmth and emotional depth. There's none of the vocal straining that would later appear on *Under Wraps*, but Ian still sings like he means it.

Instrumentally, the use of keyboard technology, piano, and real flute during the long 1:40-minute pre-vocal intro is exceptional, creating a perfect "harmony." The stunning melody, one of the best from Ian and Peter, builds the tension beautifully in anticipation of the vocals. Peter-John Vettese superbly complements Ian, both in his songwriting and his keyboard contributions on this track.

The song was performed live on several occasions, starting with an orchestral performance on German TV for an event called *The Atlas Circus*. This was a Jethro Tull presentation, where former Tull member David, now Dee Palmer assisted with the orchestral arrangements, while Ian performed in a formal suit and tie — the only time, to my knowledge, that Ian, the hippy, minstrel, vagabond, and dandy, ever dressed in such a manner.

The second performance took place back in England on the *Leo Sayer Show* on the BBC, where solo Ian gave a memorable performance, miming to the song. His presence on the same show undoubtedly overshadowed Leo's own musical efforts.

Additionally, the song was performed live during the *Under Wraps* Jethro Tull tours in late 1984. There's an excellent-quality YouTube video from the Capitol Theatre concert in the USA on 28th October, where Ian sings beautifully, with no sign of the vocal problems that would later affect him. Martin Barre joins Ian, doubling up on some of the flute riffs. Martin is clearly enjoying himself, bouncing up and down while adding electric guitar to a track that originally had no guitar in the studio version.

It's a fascinating "what might have been" scenario — had "Fly By Night" been released by Jethro Tull rather than Ian Anderson as a solo project, it could have sold millions!

This is definitely a wonderful hidden gem for me. Had it received the *Songs From The Wood* treatment, with acoustic guitar, mandolin, and more flute, and been included on a Jethro Tull album, I suspect it would have made its way into many people's top 50 Ian Anderson songs. It certainly would be in mine.

Score 15/20

Made In England *(Anderson/Vettese)*

I can't claim to always understand Ian's lyrics, and this song is no exception! It seems to narrate the life of an Englishman as it weaves through "England's green and pleasant land." Brunel earns an honourable mention, alongside three English cities —

Newcastle, Leeds, and Birmingham. My favourite line is "born each side of a dry stone mile," which is likely a nonsensical lyric. Unless, of course, it implies a father playing away and having children with different women across Yorkshire parish boundaries — a rather cheeky notion!

There is, however, an undertone of sadness in the lyrics, as England in 1983 appears to not quite be all it is cracked up to be. Perhaps not much has changed, as these lyrics could just as easily have been written for 2025.

Another intriguing thought I have about this song is that it might be about Gerald Bostock. By 1983, Gerald — eleven years on from *Thick As A Brick* (1972) — would be 19 years old, politically aware, and starting to understand the realities of England's "green and pleasant land." Could it all be about Gerald?

I doubt I'll email Ian to ask. However, we will encounter the hypothetical Gerald again in *Thick As A Brick 2* (2012) and *Homo Erraticus* (2014), where he is resurrected to provide lyrics. Perhaps Gerald's story is far from over.

Musically, the song begins with more keyboard motifs in the intro, accompanied by some electric guitar and flute that feel almost Tull-like — until the drum machine enters, sounding utterly... diabolical! Despite the drumming's shortcomings, the lively intro remains surprisingly toe tappable. At 1 minute 20 seconds, Ian's restrained yet classy vocals take centre stage. Around the 2½-minute mark, there's a pause featuring some flute flourishes before the song picks up again, continuing on its merry way with distinctly unmerry lyrics.

The song was also performed live during the *Atlas Circus* TV event in Munich. This rendition was nearly identical to the studio version but included some extra breathy, trilling flute. Ian Anderson, ever the showman, hams it up by sitting at a desk, answering the phone, and weaving theatrically through the orchestra — all while donning a very smart suit and tie.

This track stands as a hidden, if middling, gem from Ian and Peter. It's unlikely to have been performed live beyond this occasion and is even less likely to feature in future performances. Personally, I quite like the song. I might revisit it every now and then — perhaps once every decade. Still, it's far more than just album filler. Given the choice, I'd rather play this than anything from Mick Jagger's solo albums. Apologies, Mick!

Score 12/20

Walk Into Light *(Anderson)*

I have a real fondness for the lyrics on this one. The first verse seems to capture the rush of adrenaline a performer feels at the start of a gig — stepping onto the stage, bathed in light, and basking in the unconditional love of the audience. It's a joyful depiction of that moment. I doubt Ian Anderson, even now in his late 70s in 2025, has ever lost the thrill of live performance. He's certainly not alone in that — Mick Jagger and Van Morrison are two other prime examples of ageing legends who still can't resist the lure of the stage. No doubt they subscribe to Van's iconic phrase, "It's too late to stop now," which feels particularly apt for us more, shall we say, "age-challenged" types.

"Walk Into Light" is very much grounded in the present. In the second verse, Ian proclaims, "you can do it for your health," a nod to the invigorating effects of live performance — or any activity that fuels your passion. I especially love the reference to "super-troopers" in the same verse. Could it be that Ian was a secret ABBA fan all along? Don't worry, Ian — your secret's safe with me!

The third verse broadens the scope, addressing all of us mere mortals who aren't rock stars. Whether we're heading to discos, parties, or, on good hair days, even the circus, Ian's words remind us to seize those moments. These lyrics stand out as some of the most positive Ian has ever written — though, knowing him, that optimism won't necessarily carry through the rest of the album.

The music here is notably absent of any flute, with only some chording on the electric guitar scattered throughout. Around the 2:15 mark, there's a clear opportunity where a flute could have added depth, but instead, Ian opts to "de-dee" his way through the section. Is this a missed opportunity, a creative cop-out, or simply artistic licence? I'll leave that for you to decide.

A similar approach is taken in "Looking For Eden," where Ian whistles instead of playing the flute. These moments seem to reflect his desire to innovate and experiment — why not try something unexpected? In my view, this creative choice works well in both "Walk Into Light" and "Looking For Eden." It adds a layer of unpredictability to the tracks.

Of course, for those longing for a flute-centric experience, Ian's next solo album, *Divinities: Twelve Dances With God*, more than makes up for it, with the flute returning and trilling big time.

I'd argue that "Walk Into Light" is a standout gem on the album — the only track featuring genuinely positive lyrics. The more I listen to these songs, the more I can imagine them being reimagined in a "from the wood" style arrangement, with acoustic instruments and, naturally, a flute solo. What a transformation that would be!

Score 14/20

Trains *(Anderson/Vettese)*

"On trains, on trains, I seem to spend my life on trains," sings Ian Anderson. I wish I could say the same — I do rather enjoy trains. However, our North Essex village lost its station in 1963, and the nearest one is now several miles away. Unlike Ian, though, I've passed my driving test, so for me, it's more a case of, "in cars, in cars, I spend my life in cars."

This track marks Ian Anderson's third "train song." The second is "Journeyman" from Jethro Tull's *Heavy Horses* album, which delves into the mundane reality of rail commuter life but elevates it with the kind of rich, thought-provoking lyrics that define that record. The song's syncopated rhythm cleverly evokes the movement of a train journey, giving it a distinctly locomotive feel.

The first train-themed song, of course, is an obscure deep cut from *Aqualung*. Lyrically, it uses the metaphor of a runaway train to explore the unstoppable force of geometric population growth. Musically, it features a driving riff that might remind you of "Blockbuster" by Sweet or "The Jean Genie" by David Bowie, making it irresistibly foot tappable. For those so inclined, it even invites a spot of headbanging. Add to that its memorable piano intro and a flute solo that's nothing short of sublime, and you have a track for the ages. It is called "Locomotive Breath."

I wonder — have you heard of it?

"Trains" is perhaps not in the same league as Ian Anderson's earlier train-themed tracks but does share lyrical similarities with "Journeyman." Like its predecessor, it portrays the humdrum of commuter life, describing Ian's interactions with friends "at the end of the day," typically on the 17:30 train. If you're heading to the "office party," however, you'll need the 18:05 — though you'll have to hope "they take you alive from the train." It feels like a companion piece to "Journeyman" but with less engaging, more literal lyrics that lack metaphorical depth.

Musically, the track plop, plods along rather than benefiting from the syncopated rhythm that made "Journeyman" so evocative. The drum machine here, predictably, is no match for Barrie Barlow's dynamic drumming on *Heavy Horses*. Its monotonous thudding may reflect the routine and drudgery of commuting, but it doesn't make for exciting listening. The absence of guitars or flutes is notable, leaving the song awash with keyboards, and you can't help but wish someone would pull the plug out of the diabolical drum machine.

While "Trains" bears little resemblance to "Locomotive Breath," it feels uncomfortably close to "Journeyman" in both sentiment and musicality, albeit clearly inferior in both lyrics and execution. The lack of syncopation and the uninspiring percussive track are issues common to the whole album, courtesy of that dreaded drum machine. If "Journeyman" from *Heavy Horses* had never existed, "Trains" might have stood alone as an acceptable exploration of commuter life. However, by comparison, it feels weaker and less impactful.

It's perhaps no surprise that "Trains" has neither been performed live by Ian Anderson nor is likely to be in the future. Whisper it quietly, but this might be one of the weaker tracks on the album.

Score 9/20

End Game *(Anderson)*

Music often juxtaposes cheerful upbeat melodies with sombre or introspective lyrics, creating a fascinating contrast. A classic example is "Help!" by The Beatles, where John Lennon's cry for assistance, spurred by the pressures of fame, when he is "feeling down," is concealed beneath an energetic and cheerful tune. This emotional dissonance is heightened by Lennon's seemingly carefree performance on *Top Of The Pops* clips, which belies the song's deeper meaning. For a more poignant interpretation, one need only listen to Tina Turner's melancholy rendition of "said song," which brims with pathos and raw emotion, laying bare the song's deeper sentiment.

Now, let's turn to Ian Anderson, who brings his unique perspective to the theme of death in "End Game." Cheerful melodies paired with dark lyrics are not new territory for Ian. Back in "Life Is A Long Song," he wrapped a stark reflection on mortality — the punchline "the tune ends too soon for us all" — in seemingly light-hearted lyrics. This penchant for intertwining brightness with existential gloom resurfaces in "End Game." Here, death looms large, but Anderson offers a twist: the tantalising notion of a "re-match in warm snow," suggesting fun, metrological heavenly conditions for the recently departed. It's a fleeting glimmer of hope, but ultimately, the song concludes with a wave goodbye in the final verse.

Is Ian being earnest, or is the entire song a subtle exercise in p**** taking? Perhaps it's both. Anderson's knack for crafting songs with layered meanings encourages reflection as much as they entertain. "End Game" invites listeners to ponder its themes while delivering an engaging melody — a hallmark of Ian's ability to weave profundity and playfulness into his music.

The instrumental arrangement for "End Game" is dominated by synthesisers, with a drum machine attempting — perhaps ambitiously — to mimic the sound of castanets. While the melody carries a cheerfully melancholic tone, one might question whether a song about death should lend itself to being quite so foot-tapping, particularly when driven by the relentless beat of a drum machine. There are also faint hints of electric guitar woven into the track. Interestingly, I've noticed more electric guitar on this album than I initially thought. Well done, Ian — though one wonders if Martin Barre might have raised an eyebrow at its inclusion and his exclusion.

As the "end game" of the song draws near, there's a subtle but noticeable quickening of the pace, giving the impression that the inevitable conclusion is hurtling closer. The song finishes abruptly, leaving a sense of finality fitting to its theme. Thankfully, however, Ian carries on — singing, strumming, knob-twiddling, and trilling his way into side two of the vinyl, much to our collective relief.

Score 11/20

Black and White Television *(Anderson)*

Side two continues the album's trend of grim lyrical themes, and this track is no exception. Black-and-white television seems to serve as a metaphor for a life lacking vibrancy and definition — unfulfilled and devoid of colour... or so it seems. "The screen never lies" could, in a modern 2025 context, easily be repurposed as a commentary on the Internet. The lyrics are thoroughly bleak and miserable, with no glimmer of hope or optimism to be found.

This pervasive sense of despair extends across the album as a whole, reflected not only in its lyrics but also in the predominantly black-and-white album cover and sleeve design. Looking back at Tull's *Songs From The Wood* and *Heavy Horses*, their covers, lyrics, and music were rich in colour — green being particularly dominant — and imbued with a sense of optimism and celebration. By contrast, this album exudes a grey, downbeat atmosphere.

Perhaps the hard-edged, mechanistic nature of the keyboard technology used throughout contributed to the overall sombre tone, dampening any potential for lyrical brightness. Yet, in certain moments on the album, the keyboards display genuine warmth and a remarkable "sparkle," for which Peter-John Vettese deserves considerable credit. It's this contrast that keeps the album from feeling entirely devoid of light, even in its darkest moments.

The track opens with more artificial, synthesised sounds, accompanied by Ian's understated vocals, creating a pleasant enough instrumental piece. Once again, I can clearly imagine where a flute might have added texture, though this remains wishful thinking. Not that I am entirely obsessed with hating the drum machine (of course not!), but what I miss most at this stage of the album is the presence of real drums — particularly those played by Barrie Barlow.

Barrie's drumming brought syncopation, swing, and even a touch of funk, which would have added so much vitality here. Even Gerry Conway's more straightforward approach would have been a vast improvement over the nasty drum machine, which, on this track, sounds like it's suffering from indigestion. How I long for just one proper paradiddle from Barrie or Gerry to inject some much-needed life into proceedings.

Before I spiral into despair over the early 1980s cult of the drum machine, it's time to move on to the next track — a song that uses a type of food as a metaphor for, well... sex!

Score 10/20

Toad In The Hole *(Anderson)*

Toad in the hole is essentially a dish of sausages cooked in Yorkshire pudding batter, with the sausages representing a toad peering over a wedge of batter. It's traditionally served with onion gravy. As for the sexual connotations of "toad in the hole," I must admit they completely escape me.

In the song, a very lucky lady awaits her partner's return after a hard day's work, anticipating a night of luxury with "deep pile carpets" and "some fine wine to cool." However, in reality, the poor chap lives in a bedsit, relying on his imagination, and instead of a romantic evening, he's left to warm up a toad in the hole dish for his supper — hardly the scenario of being the "toad in the hole" for his lady love. Just when the lyrics are about to take a fun turn, they take a sharp left in the punchline, ending in bed sit non-heaven.

I think some of Ian's best lyrics on this album can be found in this particular song.

Musically, the track opens with guitar and sparkly keyboards, followed by piano and smooth string synthesisers. It creates a surprisingly warm atmosphere, and Ian's understated vocals add a certain charm. This is definitely one of the album's gems — likely in the top 10, though perhaps towards the lower end of the top 5.

Score 13/20

Looking For Eden *(Anderson)*

The word "Eden" is derived from a Hebrew term meaning "place of pleasure." It is commonly thought of as a paradise on Earth, where we could all live happily ever after. In its traditional sense, it refers to the most wonderful garden, filled with the finest food, lush greenery, and beautiful flowers — until Adam and Eve were expelled for disobeying God.

In the modern world, as far as the UK is concerned, "Eden" also refers to the Eden Project, an artificially created biome in Cornwall, designed to simulate a tropical rainforest. This popular tourist attraction draws millions of visitors each year.

Additionally, "Eden" was the first name of a highly useful Chelsea footballer from a few years ago, who went on to gain significant fame. I can't quite recall his name, but I suppose I could "Hazard" a guess... Oh dear, was this meant to be a serious book?

In this introspective song, Ian Anderson's vision of Eden remains elusive and nebulous, perhaps "somewhere on the edge of town." When he does find it, he dreams of tending to it, "weeding and hoeing," and living happily ever after with his "Eve." Yet, this is another song steeped in sadness and melancholy, with no resolution by its end — Eden "isn't really there at all" and cannot be found, at least not on this occasion. Perhaps not ever. Well, not until the final verse of the last track on Ian's solo album *Homo Erraticus* — "Cold Dead Reckoning" (see Chapter 6). There, we might just catch a glimpse of a chance to find our own Eden.

Everybody needs their own Eden — a place of safety, a personal sanctuary where one can find fulfilment, love, good health, and inspiration. It would be a haven for "fairy tales, shepherds, and wise men," a world away from the hustle of Oxford Street and London. In reality, Ian and his family may have found their own Eden on "their little rock island, their little patch of sand," as he described in the song "Rock Island" from Jethro Tull's 1988 album of the same name, when they moved to the Isle of Skye in 1978.

Meanwhile, "Looking For Eden" remains a sad, almost tear-jerking song, with bleak, unfulfilled lyrics that contrast poignantly with its haunting, beautiful melody.

The synth strings, choir arrangement, and cascading keyboard notes give the song a near "rock out" feel, though it never quite reaches that point. The mid-song whistling and "dee-deeing" add further layers of resigned melancholy, enhancing the pathos of the already sad lyrics.

I do wish Ian had re-recorded this without the intrusive stabbing bass line, though credit must go to Peter-John Vettese for his superb keyboard arrangement. In my view, this is one of the most hauntingly beautiful melodies Ian has ever written. I'm sure it was originally composed on acoustic guitar, and if you're interested in a possible acoustic version, check out Stewart Wood's performance on YouTube from his *Daily Sporran* shows. Stewart's acoustic reinterpretations of Jethro Tull and Ian's music are brilliant, with "Looking For Eden" in particular being utterly stunning, full of emotional resonance. Stripping away the electronic bombast reveals a truly wonderful song — another absolute gem!

Score 18/20

User Friendly *(Anderson/Vettese)*

If this track were written today in 2025, it would likely be about the Internet and its associated dangers. However, back in 1983, a digital computer interface journey sounded like fun — until you realise that, as Ian Anderson is the writer, there's an air of menace lurking beneath the surface. "I'm user friendly and I'm only stealing your mind because I am one of the boys" suggests you might want to keep a wide berth if Ian's playing on his QWERTY keyboard, as you may not come out the other side alive. As with many songs on this album, it has a distinctly bleak feel.

At the time, the hi-tech lyrics would have been very trendy in the early eighties. Ian, always keen to keep up with new musical technology, was no stranger to the latest advancements. With help from keyboard experts such as David (now Dee) Palmer, Eddie Jobson, and Peter-John Vettese, he had embraced the complex wiring, dials, buttons, and visual display units that cluttered the studio in 1983 — completely overshadowing the acoustic guitar and flute that were relegated to the corner of the room. Given this environment, "User Friendly" seemed like a fitting metaphor and song title for that time.

Ian and Peter venture into disco territory with the rhythm track, though the poor drum machine — whether old or new — struggles to keep up with the plodding bass riff, which is presumably played by a robot. However, the keyboard hooks are warm and sparkling, providing some welcome brightness. There's also a hint of flute that appears mid-song, adding some delicate trilling for decoration.

This track is very much a middling effort on the album. It would have sounded much better with a real human drummer, someone a fraction of a micro-second behind the beat, adding a touch of mistiming and all. Fortunately, the final track on the album is something special.

Score 11/20

Different Germany *(Anderson/Vettese)*

This is another song very much of its time, with lyrics that now feel somewhat outdated. On the other hand, perhaps they remain just as relevant today. The rise of the militarised far right in Germany, both then and now, has been a constant concern since World War II.

Ian's lyrics offer a snapshot of his observations in 1983. As with many of the songs on this album, the lyrics are bleak, but the good news is that, 41 years later, while the far-right threat persists, Germany remains a strong and functioning bastion of social democracy — at least for now?

However, it is the tune and melody that really shine here, standing out as some of the best on the album. The sparkling keyboard intro is complemented by a thudding bass line and powerful piano chords. Ian's singing on this track is exceptional — some of the best he's ever done, full of tonal richness, precision, and emotion, carrying the great melody effortlessly.

At 3:07, there's a stunning instrumental break where Peter-John Vettese demonstrates he has some of the quickest keyboard fingers this side of Rick Wakeman. The track concludes with a shimmering descending glissando on the piano, bringing the vocals back in. Truly impressive — take a bow, Peter-John Vettese!

Score 16/20

***

It has been fascinating to revisit all these songs after years of neglect. I think there are four absolute gems: "Fly By Night," "Walk Into Light," "Looking For Eden" (the best), and "Different Germany." The rest of the tracks are perfectly fine, but these top four, if rearranged with real drums, flute, and acoustic guitar, could have been Tull classics on an alternative album in another universe. "Looking For Eden" might even be among my top few all-time Ian Anderson tracks — it could have been even better with some more instrumentation "from the wood."

My criticism of too much drum machine and too little flute and acoustic guitar doesn't mean this is a bad album. The album was deliberately crafted this way to be different from what had come before.

In 1986, Neil Young released *Landing On Water*, a "synthy" album that had been in the works for a few years, which sparked similar sentiments as being most un "Neil like" in style. Ian's subsequent solo albums have been far more predictable, with familiar elements like flute playing, acoustic songs, or slices of prog rock.

By 2025, it's clear you now get what it says on the tin with either a traditional Neil Young or Ian Anderson/Jethro Tull album or concert.

Walk Into Light could best be described as a fascinatingly flawed album, very much of its time — experimental, worthy of critical appraisal, and brilliant in places. I won't wait another 30 years before listening to it again!

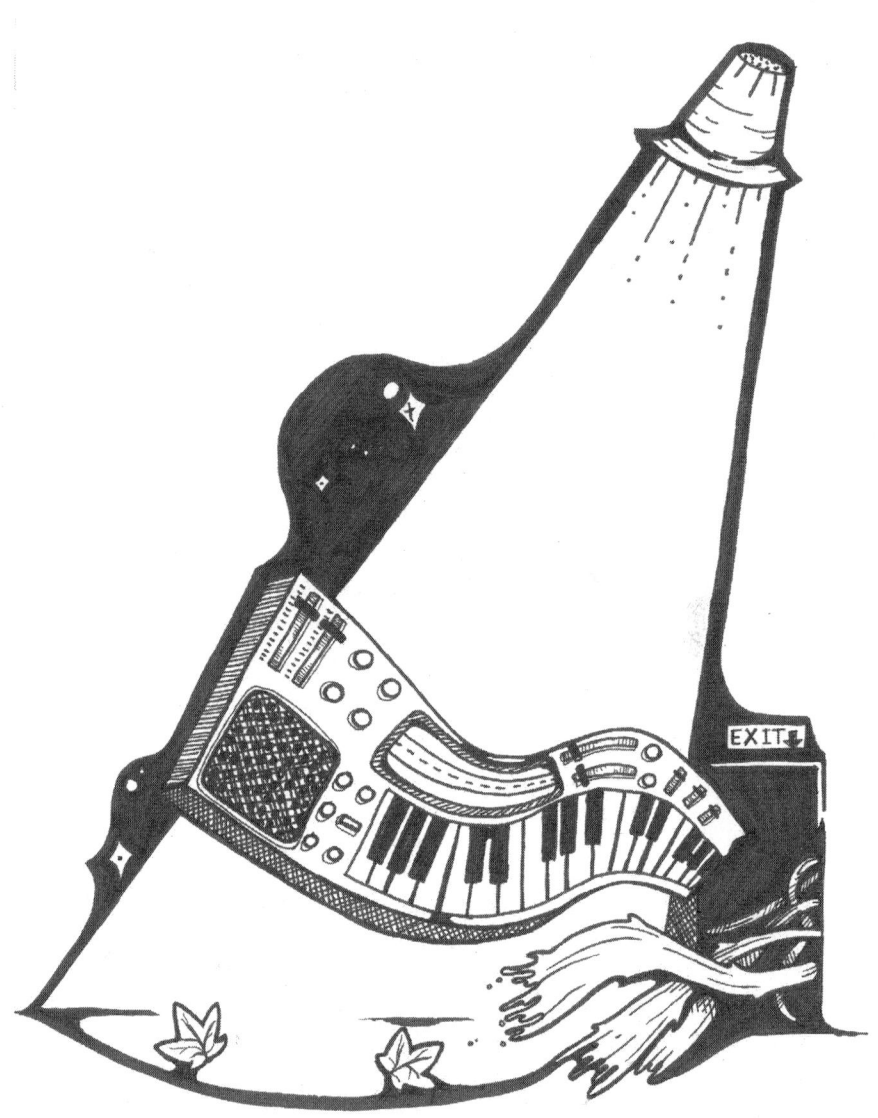

2
Divinities:
Twelve Dances With God

And now for something completely different, well, up to a point. Much like *Walk Into Light*, with Peter-John Vettese, Ian received musical support from Jethro Tull's current 1995 keyboard player, Andy Giddings. This collaboration was credited as "Additional Music" on the CD cover, with the now classically and formally labelled Andrew Giddings. He employed a vast array of 90s hi-tech keyboards to create orchestral and classical motifs, hooks, and backdrops to Ian's lead melodies. However, this time, the melodies were not sung by Ian but were instead played on various flutes, which gently permeated through and blended with the "orchestral" keyboard parts.

As with *Walk Into Light*, there was no acoustic guitar, and the album was far from the expected Ian Anderson solo effort (sensitive, acoustic, singer-songwriter with flute). Once again, the album struggled to find a wide audience, and like its predecessor, *Divinities* was not a big seller. Nevertheless, both albums feature some wonderful "Andersonesque" lead-line melodies, whether orchestrated or trilled. Ultimately, however, the comparisons stop there — one album felt like Thomas Dolby, while the other was more akin to James Galway!

Divinities: Twelve Dances With God is a classical album, or more precisely, a classical crossover album with Celtic, Eastern, and African melodic influences. It aims to represent musical motifs that evoke different world religions across cultural and ethnic divides, all united by the universal theme of oneness with a God of your choosing... perhaps? On the other hand, it could simply be a collection of pleasant flute tunes.

In terms of high culture, it is a virtuosic flute album, where Ian plays concert and alto flutes, bamboo flute, other wooden flutes, and whistles (according to the CD sleeve). There are no lyrics, and the album was created at the request of the record company, EMI. Only Ian Anderson — albeit twelve years apart — could produce two completely different solo albums in style, sentiment, and content.

Divinities: Twelve Dances With God is particularly unique because of its heavy emphasis on multiple flute performances and the absence of lyrical vocals throughout the entire album. This is something not found in any of the nearly thirty albums of original material Ian Anderson has been involved with, whether with Jethro Tull or solo, in terms of writing, producing, and performing. Personally, I quite enjoy it and consider it a stunningly brilliant album, one that I still play regularly.

Divinities: Twelve Dances With God, as Ian and Andrew often recount, came about when Roger Lewis, Head of EMI's Classical Division, sought to release new classical music that deviated from the traditional, not composed by a seriously deceased figure or performed by a massive orchestra.

He was looking for a fresh perspective and a sideways angle, a modern twist on classical music. Naturally, Ian couldn't resist the challenge, particularly since he had recently relearned how to play the flute "properly" in a classical finger style. This was after receiving feedback from his daughter Gael, who pointed out that her world-famous flautist Dad wasn't placing his fingers correctly and had been improvising his technique. As a result, Ian spent time learning to play the flute in the "James Galway" style.

In addition, Ian had acquired some bamboo flutes from India, which he was enjoying playing and which infused his music with a mystical Indian flavour. This influence would be evident not only on *Divinities* but also on the subsequent Jethro Tull album *Roots To Branches*. It was the perfect moment for a high-brow, cultured project.

However, for it to succeed, Ian needed the help of Andy Giddings, who, to suit the occasion, would adopt the more serious high brow, classical musician name of "Andrew Giddings." He was tasked with recreating the sound of an orchestra using keyboards.

Thus, *Divinities* was set to become Ian's definitive flute statement over his long career. To elevate the "arty" and cultural significance even further, the music was to be imbued with religious overtones, exploring comparative religions through its melodies and motifs.

The album was put together during late 1994 and early 1995, with Ian working on some flute melodies and basic musical structures, which he then passed on to Andrew. His task was to enhance these foundations by adding orchestral elements using his extensive collection of sampled keyboards. Ian and Andrew were so pleased with the authenticity and completeness of the resulting demos that they decided to use them nearly as they were for the finished album, adding only a few real instruments played by flesh and blood classical musicians and one rock drummer.

These are Douglas Mitchell on clarinet, Christopher Cowie on oboe, Jonathan Carey on violin, Nina Gresin on cello, Dan Redding on trumpet, and Tull's very own Doane Perry on tuned percussion (likely a xylophone) and untuned percussion (ranging from bass drums to castanets). Two further musicians, Randy Wigs on harp and Sid Gander on French horn, may not really exist, being mythical figures, with a legendary status akin to the dubious Mr Gerald Bostock from *Thick as a Brick*.

After extensive Internet trawling, I've found no trace of "musos" of those names, which suggests they may have been invented for their whimsical or humorous effect. The sleeve notes, written by Ali Aziz of the *Mesopotamia Sun Times*, also contribute to the album's light-hearted moments. I had the pleasure of meeting Ali once during a book-signing tour in the Middle East.

Listening to the album now, as then, it can be tricky to distinguish the sampled orchestral keyboard sounds from the real instruments, except, of course, for the ever-present flute.

The album was to feature twelve instrumental pieces, each with religious themes, which I will explore further in the individual track reviews. This led to Ian Anderson's choice of the title *Divinities*, which clashed with EMI's preferred title, *Twelve*

Dances With God. In a hot potch compromise, both titles were combined to create the rather long and convoluted *Divinities: Twelve Dances With God*. The result certainly sounded highbrow, cultured, and like a clever marketing ploy aimed at attracting a sophisticated punter with an interest in classical, rock, new age, Celtic, and religious music.

Unfortunately, it didn't manage to attract the anticipated crowd. It did, however, reach number one on the American *Billboard* Classical Crossover Chart — "whatever that the **** that was," as Ian cheekily remarked to audiences during the subsequent tour. Despite this, it could hardly be called a commercial success.

Personally, and I think in the ears of others, the album can be seen as an artistic triumph, making it very worthy of review and analysis.

The best way to describe the reaction from both fans and critics is bemusement, much like the reaction to *Walk Into Light* in 1983. Could this be the same man who, just a few years earlier, had won a Grammy for *Crest Of A Knave* as part of Jethro Tull, an album that was firmly in the heavy metal/hard rock genre? Yes, it definitely could.

Ian Anderson had never been easy to pin down over the years; the one certainty was to expect the unexpected from him. After *Divinities*, however, his solo work became more conventional, with acoustic flute albums and Tull-like prog rock offerings.

An Ian Anderson Band toured the entire *Divinities* album in May and June of 1995, performing the tracks in CD order across 18 shows in Europe and North America. The personnel for this tour included Ian on flutes, Andrew Giddings on keyboards, and Doane Perry on percussion. Chris Leslie, who had previously been with Whippersnapper and Fairport Convention, joined on violin (a recommendation from Tull bassist Dave Pegg). Jonathan Noyce, a newcomer and soon to be Tull bassist, stepped in after Dave was unavailable. Martin Barre, however, was absent from the line-up, and had he attended, it would have been a Jethro Tull concert rather than an Ian Anderson solo performance. For the London concert, Martin opted out, finding it strange to see the band play re-arranged Tull songs without his live guitar presence during the second half.

Unfortunately, no official concert film of these shows was ever made, which is a shame, as the grainy footage available on YouTube from a Montreal concert on 3rd June 1995, still sounds and looks impressive. With one notable exception, it's unlikely that the album's tracks have been performed live since.

"In The Grip Of Stronger Stuff," track 4 from the album, was frequently dedicated by Ian to Dave Pegg, who was known for enjoying a drink or three. Over the years, this track has become a fan favourite, often celebrated in live performances by both Ian Anderson and Jethro Tull.

The album cover artwork stands in stark contrast to the minimalistic design of *Walk Into Light*. Instead, it features a multicoloured, multi-faceted, multi-faith composition, designed by Bogdan Zarkowski. The image incorporates religious symbols and an Indian deity with six arms, possibly capable of playing three flutes at once. It serves as a vivid visual representation of the album's "aural" music, and I quite like it in a kaleidoscopic way.

Now, it's time to dive into an individual review of each track. It's a shame that there are no lyrics here, as I've quite enjoyed pretending to understand Ian's poetic wordsmithing in my previous Tull book and elsewhere in this one. I'll certainly make up for it in later albums, especially with *TAAB 2* and *Homo Erraticus*.

All tracks are officially credited as Ian Anderson compositions. Although Andrew Giddings provided additional music on the album, his contribution didn't quite reach the level of a full writing credit, unlike Peter-John Vettese's role in *Walk Into Light*, which is a bit of a missed opportunity.

Nevertheless, Andrew's efforts on *Divinities* are commendable, and like Peter-John Vettese before him, he deserves recognition. In the absence of lyrics, I'll do my best to explain the musical progression of each track in my non-musical way, with help from my classically trained and superior musical being wife, Linda, especially when it comes to understanding time signatures.

***

In A Stone Circle

A stone circle is exactly what its name suggests — a ring of standing stones, typically erected around 3000 BC at pagan sites across Britain and North-Western Europe. The exact reasons for their construction remain uncertain, though the most widely accepted theory is that they were built for religious ceremonies or rituals. Regardless of their purpose, creating these structures required considerable intellectual thought and immense physical labour. Some of these stone circles are large; the most famous is Stonehenge, while a slightly smaller but more intact example can be found at Avebury, both located in Wiltshire, England.

While many might consider "Dun Ringill" from Jethro Tull's *Stormwatch* album to be a companion piece to this track, it's worth noting that "Dun Ringill" refers to an Iron Age hill fort made of stone, located on the Isle of Skye, near where Ian Anderson used to live, rather than a stone circle. That said, both types of ancient stone structures — whether circles or forts — could easily be thought of as places "where the old gods play," as the lyrics of "Dun Ringill" suggest.

As with all instrumentals, does the title appropriately evoke the music it accompanies? Within moments of the track's beginning, string flourishes and the flute establish that this is a serious, thoughtful piece. The flute melody is stately and precise, conveying an air of calm and beauty, while synthetic strings and harp-like sounds provide a gentle backdrop. There are no dramatic shifts in key or time signature, but the abrupt, resounding thud of a keyboard drone at the end is a bit of a surprise. Perhaps Ian and Andrew thought we needed waking up.

Overall, the title "In A Stone Circle" is evocatively reflected in the music. I can easily imagine sitting in an actual stone circle while listening to this, contemplating serene thoughts of days long past.

The music has a hint of Celtic antiquity and flows along nicely, although the orchestral backing feels a little stiff without the "vibratoish" warmth of real strings. The ending drone remains a mystery, and some have wondered why it was included. Perhaps it was the work of our two mythical orchestral types, Randy Wigs and Sid Gander, sneaking it in when no one was paying attention. Regardless, I find myself quite fond of "In A Stone Circle." It's a solid track on the album and serves as a fitting introduction to what comes next.

Score 15/20

In Sight Of The Minaret

A minaret is a tower on a mosque, from which the call to prayer is broadcast five times a day, often through loudspeakers mounted on the minaret itself. The sound radiates across the surrounding area, inviting followers to worship. In addition to serving as a functional aspect of religious practice, minarets also act as visual symbols, representing the presence and role of Islam in the local community. Geographically, minarets are typically found in the Middle East, North Africa, and the Iberian Peninsula. Constructed from local stone, they are often adorned with intricate decoration to highlight their importance both as landmarks and as religious focal points.

But does "In Sight Of The Minaret," as a musical track, capture the essence of prayer, religion, and community?

The track begins with a gentle, tickling keyboard motif, accompanied by synthesised strings. This is followed by an orchestral harpsichord, moving alongside Ian's undulating flute melody, with a subtle hint of violin popping in here and there.

After about two minutes, the pace picks up unexpectedly, causing the listener (me, at least) to begin tapping their feet and nodding along. At this point, Ian's flute improvisation bursts into life with a torrent of trilling notes. To me, this is undeniably "classical with a capital C," more so than "In A Stone Circle," which carries a Celtic flavour.

However, does the music evoke the imagery of a minaret and the call to prayer? Does it conjure up a sense of the Middle East, North Africa, or even Iberian promise? The answer, for me, is no. While the track is undoubtedly lively and enjoyable, it doesn't carry the deep cultural or religious overtones that might be expected given the title. It's more of a cute nice little tune, something you might hum along to or tap your feet to, but it doesn't seem to capture the essence of the minaret.

That said, others might have a different interpretation. Perhaps this is the one track on the album that speaks profoundly about the human condition, and I simply don't "get" it. As with many of Ian's lyrics, there are times when I miss the deeper meanings, so perhaps I'm missing something here in the music too. While "In Sight Of The Minaret" isn't one of my personal favourites, it remains a solid track. The true gems of *Divinities* are still to come, in my view.

Score 10/20

In A Black Box

This one is a bit of a mystery. What exactly does Ian mean by "Black Box"? In scientific terms, a "Black Box" refers to a system where the input is known, and the output can be observed, but the internal process remains a mystery because it cannot be seen — it's "black." This concept is used in systems theory, computing, and mathematics, and understanding it fully often requires a brain the size of a planet.

A second type of Black Box is a flight recorder, which captures data from an aircraft, such as speed and altitude. After a crash, recovering the Black Box is crucial to determining what happened. Interestingly, the actual Black Box is often orange to make it easier to locate in the wreckage.

Alternatively, could Ian be referring to a coffin with the term "Black Box"? This is purely speculative, a wild theory without evidence, but it's one possibility. Then there's also the pop group Black Box, known for the controversial 1989 single "Ride On Time," which was riddled with debate over who actually sang on it.

However, I doubt Ian was thinking of any of these when writing and titling "Black Box"; instead, he was likely being enigmatic and mysterious in his typical "Anderson" way, leaving fans and critics like me scratching our heads. I can't seem to find any religious connection to a Black Box either.

So, what might the music suggest? The track begins with a gentle classical flute and orchestral backdrop, with a hint of xylophone or glockenspiel. The time signature is in waltz time (3/4), or for the musically inclined, it could be seen as a 6/8 time signature if you can keep up with the count. Around 1:30, percussion bursts onto the scene, and the music begins to swing. It feels like the backing includes some real players, with Doane Perry providing a playful, slightly bashful touch on the drums. Ian's flute has a stuttering quality, starting and stopping as if teasing the listener. Just when you think it's safe, the music halts — a bit of a tease, really.

So, how does "In A Black Box" fit in? As I listened, I didn't think of systems theory, flight data, a coffin, or the "Ride On Time" single. The title remains elusive and enigmatic, just out of reach for me. But, once again, I found myself enjoying the tune for what it is. Ian Anderson has an undeniable knack for crafting memorable flute melodies — just how does he do it?

Score 13/20

In The Grip Of Stronger Stuff

An absolute banger of an unhidden gem! In other words, this track is absolutely brilliant for me. As for the title, you can interpret it however you like. "In The Grip Of Stronger Stuff" could refer to the strong clench of religious devotion in the context of the *Divinities* album, but I reckon it's more likely referring to the call of strong, spiritual (as in whisky) alcoholic beverages taking over the subject of the music.

Just who is Ian referring to? When performed live, Ian often made a fun but never mean-spirited reference to Dave Pegg, Tull's bass player from 1979 to 1995, who was known for enjoying a drink or several, and who, at the time, could often be found in a cathartic state of alcoholic bliss or torpor. So, there you have it — a simple explanation: this track is about Dave Pegg... maybe?

Everything about this track is perfectly timed, with not

a single note out of place. It was even more stunning live, which I've had the pleasure of witnessing at several Jethro Tull concerts. The track starts with a "topsy-turvy" string keyboard sequence, overlaid with a wonderful Celtic jig flute melody, which eventually becomes accompanied by what sounds like castanets, giving the track a rhythmic "see-sawing" feel.

At around 1:15, Ian's wooden or bamboo flute enters over a stuttering, staccato orchestral piece. It's at this point that the Celtic jig's 4/4 time signature morphs into a more classically appropriate 3/4 waltz time for a short while — at least, that's what I'm told. The various sequences repeat, and it's all wrapped up in just 2:48 minutes, making it the shortest track on the album.

When I saw Jethro Tull perform this track live in the late 90s, Martin Barre's electric guitar added a bit of heaviness in places, while Ian and Andrew exchanged approving looks and grins throughout the performance. Ian looked like he was having a great time!

Live, the track came across as jaunty, joyous, and uplifting, and, in my view, only enhanced its reputation as one of the best tunes Ian Anderson has ever written. The audience's response was overwhelmingly positive, with cheers and applause, and it seemed to get the best reaction of all the tracks at that particular Jethro Tull concert I attended. This is a universally loved track – for me, for fans, and for critics alike, and I suspect Ian himself feels the same way.

A big shout-out is deserved for Andrew's arrangement and the orchestral backing. Oh, and I nearly forgot: Doane Perry's high-quality castanet (or is it drum ring?) playing deserves a mention as well. All in all, it's just a fantastic track!

Score 19/20

In Maternal Grace

"Maternal" evokes the behaviour of a mother towards her child in a positive, warm, loving, and tender way. Meanwhile, the provision of "Grace" reaffirms these maternal instincts with genuine care and intent. In other words, the sentiment of the track's title expresses heartfelt appreciation for the love a mother has for her child.

From a Christian perspective, it could also be seen as a reference to Mary, the Mother of God. As such, the music should feel decidedly pleasant, being very nice and just a teeny bit soppy and fey!

When I listen to this track, I'm struck by its attempt to capture the essence of a Celtic or Gaelic air — a gentle folk music instrumental ballad that's slow, expressive, and tinged with sadness. The track opens with a soft harpsichord/guitar keyboard hook, which is soon joined by a beautiful wooden flute melody, continuing with a keyboard imitation of a piano.

The music is stately, precise, plaintive, melancholy, and sensitive — perhaps just a little twee, but then, a mother's love for a child is exactly that, and it's certainly not something to be sniffed at and dismissed.

Even Ian Anderson can be a little twee from time to time, and why not? It's still remarkable that IA can release a track like this, especially considering that just a few years earlier, he was fronting "Steel Monkey" and winning a Grammy for out-rocking Metallica with Jethro Tull's *Crest of a Knave*.

Metallica, for all their heaviness, have yet to release a gentle, soothing, melodic classical piece for electric guitar and orchestra, but there's still time. In the meantime, Ian Anderson remains the epitome of ubiquitous eclecticism, always defying expectations and proving he is simply the best at not being confined to any rigid style.

Score 12/20

In The Moneylender's Temple

Three major world religions — Hinduism, Sikhism, and Buddhism — have temples as places of worship, often dedicated to performing rituals and paying homage to multiple deities. That said, it seems unlikely that a moneylender could ever be considered a god or deity, so perhaps they shouldn't have a temple of their own.

On the other hand, one might imagine a specific type

of temple dedicated to moneylenders, serving to affirm and validate their ennobled financial status in some elevated or ceremonial way.

There is, however, a biblical connection worth considering: the "Cleansing of the Temple" narrative in the New Testament Gospels. In this account, Jesus and his disciples enter a temple in Jerusalem and drive out the merchants and moneylenders, condemning them as part of a "den of thieves."

Quite right too, one might say — religious spaces should not become the playground of engorged capitalists! Perhaps (or perhaps not), this is the concept Ian Anderson had in mind when naming the track "In The Moneylender's Temple."

Musically, the piece is frenetic, featuring rapid flute runs over disjointed yet dynamic orchestral backdrops. It's written in a time signature of six beats to the bar, creating a fluid, non-plodding rhythm. At 1:49, a "churchy" organ briefly takes centre stage before Ian resumes improvising on a wooden or bamboo flute over an orchestral riff, which then transitions back to the original theme. Throughout, cello lines provide a resonant backdrop, adding depth that would have been equally suited to heavy electric guitar riffing. Despite this, I'm not aware of the track ever being performed live by Jethro Tull or Ian Anderson after 1995.

Although I quite like this track — it's far from bad — I struggle to connect the music to the title. One could, perhaps, argue that the torrent of quick-fire, trilling flute notes might symbolically inspire a money-grabbing lender to abandon their carnal financial desires, embrace spiritual enlightenment, and prepare themselves to devoutly appreciate the next remarkable track. Meanwhile "In The Moneylender's Temple" holds its own as a lively and engaging piece.

Score 15/20

In Defence Of Faiths

Faith is a deeply personal and powerful conviction — a strong belief in a religion or philosophy, held without proof that the tenets of that belief are objectively true or its sentiments verifiable. Faith often represents an unshakeable certainty that what one believes is absolutely right.

For most people, most of the time, faith is something to be admired, cherished, and defended. However, when one person's faith interferes with or undermines another's, conflict inevitably arises and the fun begins. Still, the concept of "In Defence Of Faiths" feels like something worth respecting and admiring, making it a fitting and thoughtful title for this track.

Of course, I could be entirely wrong. Perhaps Ian Anderson intended the title to defend women named Faith, celebrating their right to possess a memorable, one-syllable first name.

For all I know, the track could just as easily have been titled "In Defence of Sheilas, Carolines, or even Jethros." Nevertheless, I maintain faith (pun intended) in my interpretation — I just know I am right about this one!

Musically, the track opens with an organ and transitions into what might be one of the most beautiful flute melodies ever composed. The lead line briefly shifts to a harpsichord sound before returning to the flute, which is perhaps supported by a whistle. As the track develops, additional instruments join in, including what sounds like brass and possibly a glockenspiel, all carried forward in a stately waltz rhythm. The arrangement is simple, elegant, and highly effective, resulting in yet another memorable tune.

Does the music align with the title? Perhaps not entirely, although the organ does lend it a somewhat "churchy" quality that nods to religious faith. Overall, this is a serene and enchantingly calming piece, though if you're waiting for the album's rocker, don't wait up.

Score 15/20

At Their Father's Knee

This track narrates the story of a father imparting his wisdom, knowledge, and understanding of the world to his children. Seated at a lower level than their father, the children view him with a sense of awe and wonder, almost as though he were a God-like figure. The piece feels like a masculine counterpart to the feminine grace explored in "In Maternal Grace" three tracks earlier. But does the music reflect the weight of this paternal theme?

The track begins in a stately manner, with what seems to be a full orchestral backing accompanying a mournful flute melody. This sombre atmosphere persists until the music takes a dramatic turn about fifty seconds in, when the distinctive motif from Mars (as in Holst) bars (as in music) come in. *Mars, the Bringer of War* (from Holst's *The Planets*) makes an unmistakable appearance. This "Mars bars" moment — a cheeky but effective lift — was first coined as such by Dave Rees in the Tull fanzine *A New Day* during his 1995 review of "At Their Father's Knee." It was funny then, and it's still amusing now! That said, it's hard to deny the motif's impact, setting an intense and slightly menacing tone. It was a bit naughty for such a blatant Planet Sweet steal by Ian and Andrew.

As the track progresses, the music transitions to a gentler, more soothing section, only for the "Mars bars" theme to return with full orchestral force, perhaps accompanied by clarinet or synthesised sounds. One challenge throughout *Divinities* is distinguishing real instrumentation from synthesised elements, and this track is no exception. Following this dramatic reprise, the music softens again, completing what can only be described as a whirlwind of topsey turvey moods throughout the track.

It's a track of contrasts — a "prog rock, folk, classical, mini symphony epic" in miniature. The music does evoke the theme of children in awe of their wise, majestic father figure. This father is soothing and caring but also with the "Mars musical bars," occasionally formidable, with moments of intensity that demand respect and even a little fear. He is a man of many moods, a figure to be revered yet cautiously approached. That is until you realise on his days off, just like you, and me he might be found enjoying his favourite chocolate bar, conveniently named after the fourth planet from the Sun.

Score 14/20

En Afrique

For many rock 'n' roll fans, their first exposure to African music likely came in 1986 with Paul Simon's *Graceland*. This landmark album incorporated African musical hooks, riffs, and styles into the otherwise conventional singer-songwriter format.

Following this, Senegalese artist Youssou N'Dour, through collaborations with Peter Gabriel, Neneh Cherry, and others, became Africa's most famous and best-selling musician, further showcasing the continent's rich musical traditions.

African music is often characterised by its intricate rhythms, where multiple percussive layers are interwoven, using both tuned and untuned instruments. Additionally, a hallmark of the style is its "call and response" dynamic, where instruments or vocals engage in a lively back-and-forth exchange.

So how well did a middle-aged man from Blackpool, steeped in a pan-European Celtic and classical tradition, manage to produce music with a distinctly African influence?

This track evokes an "on safari" atmosphere, with its layered percussion and jaunty, lively rhythm — almost reminiscent of the syncopated "Bo Diddley" beat — over which Ian's wooden flute delivers light improvisation. But is it truly African in style? And, more importantly, is it any good? While the percussion elements capture an African flavour, the track lacks the instrumental call-and-response interplay that's a hallmark of the genre. The flute remains the sole lead instrument, and overall, the piece feels somewhat plain and repetitive, at least to my perhaps untrained ears.

Although not a track I would seek out regularly, it has its moments of charm. That said, it falls short of the energy and complexity that make African music so captivating. Apologies to Ian and Andrew — this one doesn't quite hit the mark for me. But the album redeems itself magnificently in its final three tracks, where things undoubtedly take a turn for the better!

Score 9/20

In The Olive Garden

Olives are small stone fruits, greenish-yellow in colour, similar in structure to cherries. They offer notable health benefits, being rich in vitamin E, which supports healthy vision and skin. Additionally, olives are high in antioxidants, known for their anti-cancer and anti-ageing properties. Whether eaten whole or consumed as olive oil, you might just live for ever and a day- they are often lauded for their contribution to longevity Olive gardens, cultivated across the Middle East, hold religious significance and are considered sacred in Judaism, Christianity, and Islam. Given this, we might anticipate a fruity musical piece with a reverential tone and a touch of Middle Eastern flavour to match the title.

The track begins with a gentle, lyrical melody, supported by the usual string backing, and an ethereal harp line, likely plucked by the enigmatic Randy Wigs. Ian's flute, with a delicate vibrato, seems to harmonise with either a violin, whistle, or possibly even a clarinet. The result is a soothing and contemplative piece — perfect for imagining oneself in a serene olive garden on a warm summer's day.

As I reflect on this track in February 2025, its serene quality is contrasted by the harsh realities faced by many in the Middle East, particularly in Palestine and Israel, regions historically abundant with olive gardens but now embroiled in conflict. This imbues the tune with a deeper pathos and a sense of sadness that perhaps was not originally intended. When Ian and Andrew composed this piece 30 years ago, they could not have foreseen its poignant relevance today, where the simple peace of an olive garden feels heartbreakingly out of reach for many.

Score 14/20

In The Pay Of Spain

Trying to decipher Ian's track titles on *Divinities* has been an entertaining challenge, but I must confess to being thoroughly stumped by this one. Typing "In the Pay Of Spain" into a search engine yielded detailed instructions on interpreting a Spanish payslip, complete with pesetas and tax deductions. Needless to say, this is almost certainly not what Ian Anderson had in mind. It may be a historical reference, but even after several minutes of dedicated research, I came up empty-handed. Thus, the title remains an enigmatic, mysterious riddle — likely comprehensible only to those in the know. Unfortunately, I'm not one of them. But what about the music? Happily, it's more straightforward — and quite impressive.

The track opens with a clarinet, castanets or maracas, and a jerky, off-beat plucked string motif. Over this, yet another of Ian's gorgeous flute melodies emerges, eventually echoed by lush synthetic strings and possibly clarinet and oboe. At 2:31, Ian teases us with a breathy, flutter-tongued, jazzy flute passage, only to quickly return to his more measured classical style. The orchestral arrangement on this track is particularly strong, with Andrew Giddings weaving various classical instrumental textures seamlessly around Ian's flute lines. There's even the occasional hint of syncopated swing.

Does the track sound Spanish? Does it evoke the flair of a spaghetti western like *The Good, The Bad and The Ugly*, famously filmed in Spain? Absolutely not. There's no trace of recognisable Spanish musical motifs here. Nonetheless, it stands out as one of the stronger tracks on the album, showcasing Andrew Giddings' exceptional skill in crafting intricate, dynamic arrangements.

Score 16/20

In Times Of India (Bombay Valentine)

The *Times of India* newspaper, established in 1838, holds the title of the largest-circulating English-language newspaper in the world, a feat made possible by India's vast population (approximately 1.2 billion in 2025) and its large English-speaking demographic (around 400 million, or 42%).

A "Bombay Valentine" sounds like it says on the tin, suggesting a gift purchased for a loved one either in Bombay or from Bombay. However, it's unlikely that Ian Anderson was referring to either newspapers or romantic gestures when composing this instrumental piece.

So, does the track evoke the essence of India or offer a sense of historical Bombay? In 1995, Bombay was officially renamed Mumbai to honour the goddess Mumba Devi, the city's patron deity. Should the track, therefore, have been subtitled "Mumbai Valentine"? These are intriguing questions, but as for whether the music answers them — probably not. Nevertheless, at 8 minutes and 9 seconds, it is by far the longest track on the album and, for many, the most impressive.

The piece unfolds in what feels like two distinct halves. It begins with rapid-fire trills on the flute layered over a "Morse code"-like single note on piano, soon accompanied by orchestral "back-and-forth" textures created with synthesised strings, winds, piano, and percussion.

Ian's ability to produce such extraordinarily fast runs on the flute is astonishing, reminiscent of a Ritchie Blackmore shredding guitar solo in its agility. Both Ritchie and Ian must have mesmerising fingers! The track meanders pleasantly through its themes until approximately the five-minute mark, at which point the music transitions into a remarkable outro.

For the final three minutes, an outstanding flute melody takes the spotlight, accompanied by a grand orchestral arrangement courtesy of Andrew Giddings. The backing adopts a "flip-flop" rhythm, gently shifting into a swing-like, almost rock-and-roll groove that is irresistibly foot-tapping.

As the piece fades into the distance, faint voices can be heard. Could it be Andrew cheekily asking Ian if he could revert to being "Andy" for the next Tull tour and album or even asking for some composing royalties? Whether or not this playful interpretation holds any truth, this track stands out as one of the finest on *Divinities*. But is it the best? Not quite — though it comes very close!

Score 17/20

**

Divinities: Twelve Dances with God is a superb showcase of Ian Anderson's remarkable flute playing, particularly in his newly developed classical style with refined fingering techniques. My musically (and in all other respects) superior wife assures me that Ian's tone on this album is pure, precise, and clear — markedly improved compared to earlier years. Not bad at all for someone venturing further into the realm of classical flute playing.

I've also listened to James Galway, and I'm told his tone is even purer, enhanced by a classical vibrato (or "wobble") that Ian seldom employs. Nevertheless, the structured and improvisational melodic flute work on *Divinities* is truly exceptional. It's fun to imagine how James Galway might fare with the iconic flute solo from "Locomotive Breath." My guess? He'd nail it — vibrato and all!

The contributions of Andrew Giddings (or, as he was previously known, Andy) must not be overlooked. His orchestration and arrangements on this album brilliantly support Ian's flute work, blending seamlessly to enhance the overall listening experience. It's arguably Andrew's finest collaborative effort with Ian and Jethro Tull, marking a high point in their creative partnership.

As for personal highlights, my favourite tracks include "In A Stone Circle," "In Defence Of Faiths," "In The Pay Of Spain," and "In Times of India." However, the absolute standout is "In the Grip Of Stronger Stuff." Bursting with energy, optimism, warmth, and sheer virtuosity, it towers above the rest. I strongly suspect that when I compile my top ten Ian Anderson tracks and songs in the conclusion of this book, "Stronger Stuff" will be right up there.

Thus far, Ian has delivered two predictably "unpredictable" albums. That, however, was about to change significantly with the next four records...

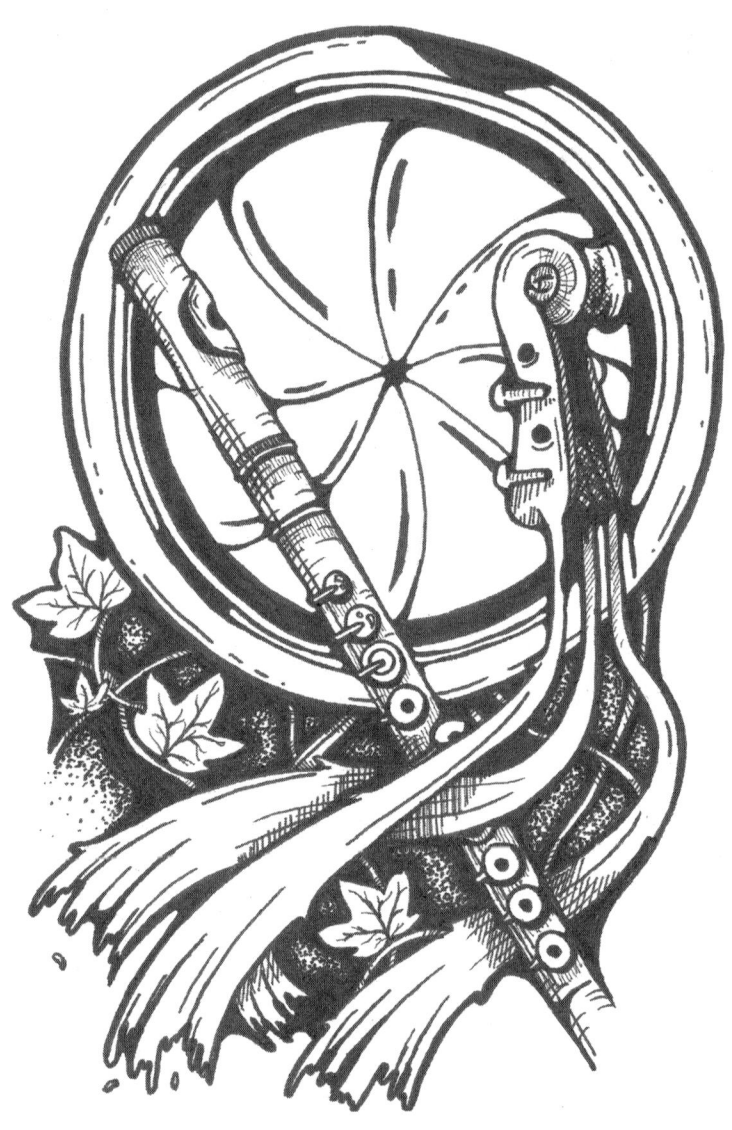

3
The Secret Language Of Birds

By the release of Jethro Tull's second album, *Stand Up* (1969), Ian Anderson had begun crafting and arranging acoustic-based songs like "Jeffrey Goes To Leicester Square" and "Look Into The Sun." These tracks were notable for their lack of rock 'n' roll bombast and absence of riff-driven electric guitar. Meanwhile, in a parallel *Stand Up* universe, the album also featured thundering eyeballs out rock pieces like "Nothing Is Easy" and "A New Day Yesterday," showcasing electric guitar prowess. This acoustic-electric dichotomy became a defining characteristic of Jethro Tull's sound.

The acoustic theme extended to the No. 4 single "Witch's Promise," released in January 1970. On *Top Of The Pops*, Martin Barre, usually wielding an electric guitar, appeared perfectly content strumming a few acoustic chords while Ian gave a spirited performance on flute and vocals.

By this time, Ian's repertoire of acoustic instruments had expanded considerably. In addition to the flute and acoustic guitar, he was adept at playing the mandolin, balalaika, bouzouki, 12-string guitar, piccolo, and whistle.

This acoustic sensibility contrasted sharply with the band's hard rock persona, driven by Martin Barre's electrifying riffs and the powerful drumming of Clive Bunker, Barrie Barlow, Mark Craney, Gerry Conway, and Doane Perry. Fans embraced this balance between delicate folk and thunderous rock, which would define Jethro Tull's sound for the next three decades.

The only other band in the 1970s to rival Tull in this electric-versus-acoustic mastery was a little-known group called Zed Leppelin. Tracks like "Stairway To Heaven" and "The Battle Of Evermore" from their fourth album epitomised this duality, much as Tull did.

By the time *Aqualung* was released, pure acoustic tracks like "Cheap Day Return," "Mother Goose," and "Slipstream" occupied roughly 25% of the album's runtime. Acoustic elements were also woven into more prominent tracks, including the title song, "Aqualung."

Over the following decades, this balance persisted, with extended prog rock epics such as "Baker St. Muse" from *Minstrel In The Gallery* and "Budapest" from *Crest Of A Knave* featuring significant acoustic interludes.

Given this history, it seemed almost inevitable that Ian Anderson would eventually release a solo album further exploring these acoustic concepts. However, Ian being Ian, he defied expectations.

Walk Into Light leaned heavily on synthesisers, while *Divinities: Twelve Dances With God* focused predominantly on flute-led instrumentals with no vocals. It took a full 17 years after his solo debut for Ian to deliver the "predictably predictable" acoustic solo album fans had always anticipated. *The Secret Language Of Birds* finally arrived in March 2000, fulfilling that long-held promise.

The recording of *The Secret Language Of Birds* (affectionately and affectedly abbreviated as SLOB) actually took place in 1998. However, its release was delayed until after the Jethro Tull album *J-Tull Dot Com*, which arrived in August 1999.

As a teaser for what was to come, the lead track from SLOB, "The Secret Language Of Birds (Part 1)," was included as a bonus at the end of *J-Tull Dot Com*. There was initial consideration given to releasing both albums simultaneously, as Ian Anderson perhaps (misguidedly) assumed that the predominantly acoustic SLOB and the primarily electric *J-Tull Dot Com* would appeal to distinct audiences.

Most Tull fans, myself included, were quite content with the staggered releases. As the saying goes, you can have too much of a good thing all at once. Had both albums been released in 1999,

I might have found myself overwhelmed and, in the eyes of my non-Tull friends — and a then non-Tull-enthusiast girlfriend — even more insufferable than usual. The gap between the albums made commercial sense, too; the inclusion of the SLOB track on the Tull album whetted appetites and built anticipation for the solo album's eventual release the following year.

Ian began developing several "proto" acoustic songs during Tull downtime in 1998. The ever-versatile Andrew Giddings, returning to lend his talents, joined Ian in fleshing out these ideas. Ian played an impressive array of instruments, including flute, acoustic guitar, acoustic bass, bouzouki, mandolin, percussion, and piccolo. The multi-talented Giddings took on nearly everything else, contributing accordion, marimba, piano, organ, electric bass, orchestral keyboards, and additional percussion. Martin Lancelot Barre, a familiar name to Tull fans, provided electric guitar on a couple of tracks, showing — unsurprisingly — his usual flair. Drumming duties were shared among Darren Moody (who had worked with Martin on his solo projects), Ian's son James Duncan, and the incomparable Gerry Conway.

Gerry Conway's contributions to SLOB are particularly poignant given his recent passing in March 2024. He was a key figure on Jethro Tull's *Broadsword And The Beast* album, added session drums to *Crest Of A Knave*, and played on two tracks for SLOB. Known for his straightforward, no-nonsense drumming style and his reputation as an all-around "nice bloke," Gerry also had a distinguished career with Cat Stevens in the 1970s and later became a long-standing member of Fairport Convention. Ian greatly valued Gerry's musicianship and character, and his loss will be deeply felt. Rest in peace, Gerry — you will be sorely missed.

The album title, *The Secret Language Of Birds*, likely refers to the morning birdsong — a sound that's utterly unfathomable to my untrained ears but nonetheless a delightful and soothing way to wake up. It could also be a broader reference to birdlife in general, whether through science, folklore, or symbolism — both in a factual sense or as part of a story.

Interestingly, two books also bear the *SLOB* title: one by Adele Nozedar (2006, non-fiction) and another by Lynn Kelly

(2024, children's fiction). The former was clearly inspired by the aural *SLOB* created by Ian Anderson, while the latter was titled as such with the encouragement of parents who were fans of Ian's work. I know this for a fact — would I lie to you?

Another theme running through the album is a subtle reference to famous artists in the lyrics, including Constable, who I am familiar with, and Rousseau, who I am not.

The album cover, designed by Bogdan Zarkowski (who also created the cover for *Divinities*), is bold, brash, and unmistakably eye-catching. It features stylised parrots in the midst of a "blue and red conversation," presumably discussing Ian's bird-song inspired flute playing.

Moving on to the individual track reviews, lyrics make a return after *Divinities*, so I'll have plenty of opportunities to pretend I know what I'm talking about when analysing Ian the wordsmith. Fortunately, Ian provides some helpful notes on the lyrics inside the album sleeve — though, of course, that's only useful if I can actually understand the words!

With synthesisers not dominating the music, nor multiple flutes, it should be easier to follow, shouldn't it? I may not have mentioned it before, but I do really enjoy this album, so this could be a fun journey!

***

The Secret Language Of Birds

The album begins, as expected, with natural birdsong. It brings to mind the opening of Yes's prog rock epic "Close To The Edge," which starts with Rick Wakeman's bird-like keyboard sounds, building up until Steve Howe's guitar riff enters. However, that's where the comparison ends.

The mood is almost a love song. I must admit, as a young, free, and single man, I never tried the chat-up line: "Stay with me and learn the secret language of birds," or, to put it another way, "If you stay over, it will be wonderful for you, but if not, the dawn chorus around here will be absolutely brilliant." It works for Ian, though; he even has a Rousseau-inspired garden out back, complete with hidden monkeys (which you can spot in

Bogdan Zarkowski's cover art), to impress his guest.

The Secret Language Of Birds is very much an occasion for Ian to name-check various artists, and the song is no exception. Rousseau, the 19th-century impressionist painter known for his jungle scenes (despite never having visited one), is referenced. By day, he worked as a tax collector. In the lyrics, monkeys, swallows, and warblers all make an appearance. What girl could resist such a colourful, impressionist garden? The lyrics are fun, vivid, and there's no sad twist at the end, which Ian sometimes does. Everyone lives happily ever after, at least until the next song.

Musically, the track is predictably led by acoustic guitar and flute, with a laid-back bass and charming drums by Gerry Conway. There are occasional hints of lead acoustic guitar and some infill piano. Ian's voice from 1998 is relaxed, clear, and sounds genuinely happy, and why wouldn't it be? If you have a Rousseau garden full of beautifully singing birds and the girl is still with you at the end of the song, life isn't too bad.

While it's not my favourite track, "The Secret Language Of Birds" (the song) is a great opener for the album. It's hummable, foot-tappable, and filled with warm, positive lyrics.

Score 13/20

The Little Flower Girl

This one could be tricky. Ian references in his notes a painting by Sir William Russell Flint titled *The Little Flower Girl, Senlis*. The painting depicts a girl sitting by a pillar in a church in Senlis, France, surrounded by flowers, while a nun passes by and looks at her.

The lyrics seem to portray Ian as a "voyeur," observing the scene and letting his thoughts wander into somewhat... shall we say, erotic territory. Well, I never!

Ian would likely argue that he was merely playing the role of the "actor" in the song, much like the nasty, pervy villain in a film who, despite being a universally loved thespian in real life, is cast in a less-than-savoury role. Ian Anderson has occasionally dabbled in this style of lyric in Tull's music, and the lyrics here could certainly be considered a little unsettling. Would he write them today, in 2025? Probably not!

Musically, I can detect mandolin, layers of guitars, orchestral keyboard sounds, organ, and possibly accordion, along with some handclaps — definitely maybe — all supporting the vocal and flute melodies. Gerry Conway contributes here, too, bringing a delicate and subtle touch to the track. There's a sudden, super-fast flute run towards the end that I really enjoy.

Over the years, I've enjoyed the song, playing it many times, but I was never really aware of the lyrics — how sad is that? The music itself sounds light, in a good way — cheerful, and is delivered well with Ian's slight speaking style. All seems fine until the slightly eerie lyrics kick in. If you ever needed to introduce Ian Anderson and Jethro Tull to a non-Tull fan, on no account should you play this song. Not even when drunk!

Score 12/20

Montserrat

The Soufrière Hills is a complex of once mainly dormant volcanoes on the Caribbean island of Montserrat, which erupted violently on 18 July 1995 after nearly 30 years of inactivity, with not even a hint of smoke beforehand.

The southern part of the island, including the capital, Plymouth, was evacuated, and by January 1996, the area was completely emptied of people. At the time, Montserrat was still a British Overseas Territory, and the UK came under criticism for not providing sufficient financial aid to help the island recover.

Around 7,000 people were evacuated, either to other parts of the West Indies or to the UK. Today, sporadic eruptions continue in the southern exclusion zone, while the northern part of the island remains habitable, with a few thousand people having returned or stayed.

Ian wrote the lyrics three years after the eruption. Like many other visitors, he had been captivated by Montserrat's stunning scenery and warm hospitality, and he felt deeply saddened by the destruction caused by the eruption.

In my view, his lyrics are exceptional. There is vivid imagery and wordplay that brings to life the sights, sounds, smells, and heat of the eruption. Ian captures the island's "anger" — both literally, through the violent and noisy eruption, and figuratively, in the sense that not enough was done politically, particularly by the UK government, to aid the island. The lyrics are descriptive, geographically specific, and tell a powerful story. They convey sadness, anger, melancholy, and irony, showcasing Ian Anderson's brilliance as a lyricist when he truly puts his mind to it.

So, does the music complement the lyrical depth and poetry? I really appreciate the lead melody, both on the flute and the vocals, which are clear and expressive. The chordal backing shifts from cheerful to sorrowful at times, enhancing the emotional range of the song. There's some impressive snare drumming, presumably performed by either Ian or Andrew, as the sleeve notes list no other drummer for this track. Unless, of course, it's a dreaded drum machine — but I sincerely hope not!

Overall, I think this is a great track. While the music occasionally leans towards being too pleasant — perhaps it should feel angrier to better match the mood of the lyrics — the true highlight is the exceptional storytelling in the lyrics, which are simply magnificent.

Score 15/20

Postcard Day

When I was a child in the 1960s, my father would attend the annual Nalgo Conferences, which were invariably held at seaside locations like Blackpool or Bournemouth. Nalgo was the local government union at the time, now defunct. He would send the most mundane postcards home, often saying things like "good view from hotel, weather's cool, see you soon."

These simple notes kept my mum happy and ensured he had clean clothes when he returned. He didn't "paint a picture" with his words, nor did he ponder the indeterminate line where the sky meets the sea, or consider the artistic quality of his postcard writing — he certainly didn't write a song about it, as only Ian Anderson could.

Just to clarify, I was perfectly content with my straight-forward boring dad. He bought me my first Beatles single ("Twist and Shout"), but he couldn't write a "mean" postcard to save his life.

The lyrics of this track feel very much like a "wish you were here" — perhaps, or perhaps not. They seem to say, "Let me describe the view in 29 lines of prose, you don't know what you're missing"... or at least that's how I interpret it. The words are a bit tricky for me on this one. Am I just a bit "thick as a brick," or do I simply lack the imagination to craft a flowery postcard? It's probably a yes to both.

The track is characterised by lots of strumming and flutey trilling, with what sounds like bongos or drums (played by Ian or Andrew?). There's also an intermittent electric and acoustic bass. The chord progression, along with the vocal and flute melodies, are pleasant enough, but "Postcard Day" doesn't quite reach the same high standards as some of the other tracks on *SLOB*. At least Ian Anderson knows how to send a decent postcard!

Score 9/20

The Water Carrier

I think the lyrics seem to depict a scene where bottled water is being sold to tourists, with the female seller flirting with the male buyer using her "black pool" eyes while seated on a Nain (oriental rug) carpet in a café. Meanwhile, Ian, in his notes, references Sir William Russell Flint (whom we encountered earlier) and Cornish artist Walter Langley, both of whom painted works titled *The Water Carrier*.

Sir William's version features a topless female figure, as one might expect, while Walter's depiction presents a more modest and respectable lady, fully clothed. Both women carry earthenware (non-plastic) porcelain pots. It's hard to say whether Ian's notes or his song lyrics for "The Water Carrier" are more intriguing, but what about the tune itself?

The song is propelled merrily and melodiously by acoustic guitar, mandolin, accordion, flute, and congas percussion, all playing at a lively pace. The album notes mention that Martin Barre plays electric guitar on this track, though it's difficult to distinguish his contribution — there are no metallic riffs or quick fire, fast triplet solos to be heard.

I've seen this song extended live during Jethro Tull concerts in the 2000s, where it was placed in the usual "Fat Man" slot. This version featured an acoustic workout for mandolin, acoustic guitar, flute, and congas, and it was very entertaining — enjoyed by all, especially Tull's drummer Doane Perry, who tapped his way to percussive heaven. "The Water Carrier" live truly elevated what was initially a solid but unspectacular studio track.

Score 11/20

Set Aside

In the late 1990s, countries within the European Union were overproducing cereal, which couldn't be sold and ended up being stored in warehouses, colloquially known as "grain mountains." In response, the EU introduced a policy that required farmers to set aside a portion of their land to leave fallow. The advantage was that farmers received a subsidy for this, and the land — up to 15% of their farm — could then be used for recreational activities like go-karting, mountain biking, or camping.

Alternatively, the land could be dedicated to nature conservation, land reclamation, or even tree planting for additional income. The policy was aptly named "Set Aside." This approach increased biodiversity, improved soil fertility, and created wider field edges for footpaths. Politicians, farmers, and the public generally considered the scheme a success, with everyone benefiting. However, as the demand for cereal increased across Europe, the policy was abandoned in 2008.

Meanwhile, if you or your family, or your farm, are "set aside" with a small 's' and 'a', it may feel like being discarded, abandoned, left out of the loop, and forgotten. You might lose your home or farm because, as a tenant, your landlord evicts you. Your once-proud farm could fall into ruin. In other words, while the EU's capitalised "Set Aside" policy was beneficial, the lower-case "set aside" can represent neglect and abandonment. This is likely the theme Ian addresses in his lyrics.

In his very brief 1.5-minute song, Ian's lyrics seem to reflect this lower-case "set aside." However, as a country dweller, Ian would have been aware of the EU "Set Aside" policy, and perhaps it influenced his choice of title, though only in a peripheral way. The song's lyrics paint a grim picture of the countryside, with "thin hedges," a "farmhouse in tatters," and, in the final line, "a landscape of tears."

The words evoke an image of an abandoned rural world, one that makes the listener long for a revival of the once-thriving farm. While it's tempting to think that Ian might be critiquing the EU's "Set Aside" policy — perhaps even making an anti-EU statement about wasting resources — I don't believe this is the main thrust of the song. Rather, I think Ian is using the metaphor of a derelict, neglected countryside to inform his lyrics.

As with many of Ian's songs, the meaning can be a little tricky and open to interpretation, but that's part of their charm. Challenging lyrics that provoke different opinions are what make his work so compelling — not necessarily something that's always clear-cut.

Musically, the song features acoustic guitar, flute, and a relaxed, easy vocal, paired with a rustic folk melody typical of Ian's style or that of Jethro Tull. Dave Rees, in his review of the *SLOB* album for *A New Day* magazine, notes that "Set Aside" reminds him of "Broadford Bazaar" from the *Heavy Horses* box set, and I agree with him. For the shortest track on *SLOB*, this song certainly has certainly got me lyrically bedazzled. It's a fun, catchy tune, and despite the wordy complexity, it remains one I enjoy to this day.

Score 11/20

A Better Moon

Albert Moulton Foweraker, the painter Ian mentions in his sleeve notes, was known for his fascination with the ethereal effects of moonlight on the night landscape. He skilfully contrasted the natural lunar light with that of lanterns and the warm glow from open windows as people meandered through the Dorset countryside (where he lived).

Ian's lyrics evoke this imagery, referencing "lamps" and "buffalo" (which haven't been found in Dorset for thousands of years) and perhaps hinting at a nocturnal romance only possible under a "Better (full) Moon." This moonlight illuminates a colourful, ethereal, and tropical setting.

The song begins by imagining Foweraker's landscape being transported 5,000 miles to "Moony" Africa, rather than sticking to a typical rainy, cloud-covered Dorset night with not much to see.

Foweraker did travel to Africa, so he may well have encountered a buffalo. This is very much an Anderson-inspired painting, where Ian draws from Foweraker's colourful legacy to create a tropical setting, blending reality with imagination. In a way, Foweraker and the other artists mentioned could arguably deserve writing credits or royalties, though Ian acknowledges them in the sleeve notes.

Musically, the track features a looping bass, acoustic guitar, subtle synth strings, and gentle flute, creating a stately, processional feel. Ian's voice carries a slightly world-weary tone, adding depth to the song. While I do enjoy it, I find it a little slow-paced and plodding for my taste. Is that a criticism? Only a small one — don't tell Ian — but overall, I still like the song.

Score 10/20

Sanctuary

Enigmatic, isn't it? Here's my (perhaps vain) attempt to explain the lyrics. The first verse seems to reference a girl sold into slavery, who eventually finds her way back to "sanctuary" — a place of safety, which in this case is Nepal.

The second verse appears to be about a cat returning to "sanctuary" after being in the "Victorian Zoo." Ian has a history of exploring both themes. The first verse reminds me of the sentiment in "Beside Myself" from Tull's *Roots To Branches* (1995), which tells the sad story of child exploitation in Bombay.

Perhaps by 1998, when *SLOB* was written, the child had been rescued by "good angels" and brought home to Nepal.

As for Ian's well-known love of cats, there are four other IA songs that touch on this theme: "...And The Mouse Police Never Sleep" from *Heavy Horses*, "Hunt By Numbers" from *J-Tull Dot Com*, and "Rupi's Dance" and "Old Black Cat" from *The Rupi's Dance* album.

So, both the child and the cat get their sanctuary... or do they? Ian adds a twist by finishing each verse with the word "waiting," implying that something more may be at play. Perhaps sanctuary isn't enough after all.

This adds layers of depth to the lyrics, exploring the human (and feline) condition. As with many of Ian's songs, whether with Tull or solo, the true meaning is left hanging just out of reach, allowing for multiple interpretations. While Ian's sleeve note says the song made him "cry," it leaves me with more of a "sigh" of bewilderment. After all those profound meteoric metaphors, it's now time to focus on the music.

Musically, "Sanctuary" is a standout track, with an excellent melody that is the best on the album so far. The acoustic guitar is beautifully complemented by the exquisite "violin" playing from Andrew Giddings, all done on a synthy, computerised keyboard. Ian's singing is tender, emotive, and sympathetic, perfectly suited to his more restrained 90s voice. Darren Mooney's drumming is subtle and sensitive, adding to the song's delicate atmosphere. There are tasteful little lead acoustic guitar breakettess throughout, and the flute comes into its own during the outro. "Sanctuary" is, without a doubt, my favourite song on *SLOB* so far, even if I don't completely understand the lyrics. It's an unhidden gem!

Score 17/20

The Jasmine Corridor

Jasmine is a cultivated plant, similar to the olive, grown in warm climates for decoration and to be used in perfumes. However, "The Jasmine Corridor" refers to a rock-climbing slab of Millstone Grit in England's Peak District, rated "E6" for climbers, which is a challenging grade. Ian Anderson was a well-known rock climber and adventurer, and it's suggested that he wrote a song about his first ascent of this particular climb. Or perhaps it's just a false news story...

Back in the world of Ian Anderson, the internationally acclaimed rock star and introspective songwriter, "The Jasmine Corridor" could symbolise the journey of life, from youthful beginnings to death, all within the span of 3:54 minutes. Alternatively, it might represent a "stairway to heaven," a transition from this world to the next.

Regardless, the song is romantic and reflective, evoking an "all my life" kind of feeling. It's quintessentially "Andersonesque" in its thoughtfulness, with a bittersweet ending. In the song, the narrator is accompanied throughout life by the girl of his dreams, even to his deathbed, where he observes the "final view from the jasmine corridor," surrounded by his cats and grandchildren.

As a lyricist, Ian is often preoccupied with themes of death, which frequently seems to loom near the end of many of his songs. Yet in "The Jasmine Corridor," the lyrics are so evocatively reflective that they resonate deeply. I absolutely love the words to this track!

Musically, the song begins with acoustic guitar, bass, organ, and "squeeze box" accordion. Ian's vocals are plaintive, melancholic, and yearning, which suits the track perfectly. The song is quite lively, especially with the addition of tambourine percussion.

Interestingly, no one, not even Ian, plays the flute in this song. For me, it's a beautiful tune with exceptional lyrics. After this, we could certainly use a more upbeat song with plenty of flute and a catchy melody. Thankfully, that's exactly what's coming next — time to "reel" in the next "spicy" track (oh dear)!

Score 15/20

The Habanero Reel

The Habanero is one of the hottest and spiciest peppers around. While the Carolina Reaper is technically hotter, it is a crossbreed that incorporates elements of the Habanero, with a similar fiery intensity. Essentially, to eat a Habanero, you need to be a tough person, prepared to sweat and foam at the mouth as you chew. Meanwhile, a reel is a folk dance and tune originating from Scotland, typically in 4/4 or 2/4 time. Unlike a jig, which has three fast notes between each beat, a reel has four.

So, the backstory of this "very warm" song seems to be about dancing a reel while eating the hottest pepper this side of the Milky Way, accompanied by "rum and cola," "ears of bat," and "eye of eagle," and somehow surviving to the end of the 4:01-minute track to play the next song. Good luck with that! But it certainly sounds like fun.

At last, we have a cheerful, lively song with great lyrics and a wonderful tune — an excellent antidote to some of the heavier, more intense songs that came before it. The flute and accordion double up on the main melody, with acoustic guitar backing, and Ian even has a rare outing on piccolo. The vocals flow effortlessly and are just as entertaining when sung as they are when read on paper. The overall tune is jaunty, lively, and, well, "reely" (sorry!) good. It's syncopated, foot-tapping, and perfect for playing air flute — it truly kicks a***! This track is another absolute gem, one that gets straight to the taste buds.

Score 17/20

Panama Freighter

Panama is the southernmost country in Central America, just north of South America. Put that into your sat-nav, and it will take you to the ocean-bound "Panama Freighter," leaving from Southampton Docks on a romantic journey across the "lumpy sea."

Nearly 9,000 ships and freighters (around 16% of the world's total) fly the Panama flag, as the country is known for its lax regulations regarding health and safety. However, Panama benefits financially from this "flag of convenience," even though the "Panama Freighter" may not actually visit its namesake country. It's possible to be a paying passenger on a cargo freighter, which could offer a magical, solitary experience

— a journey of redemption and reflection for the weary traveller rushing through life.

Alternatively, you could meet the girl of your dreams (not the one from "Sanctuary") in a shantytown, and then head home on the rusty brown "Panama Freighter" to live happily ever after. This creates quite a romantic encounter in Ian's lyrics, which (I assume) has a happy ending, with no break-up or death at the end of the song. While the lyrics are enjoyable, the real highlight is the tune itself, which is something special.

Yes, I absolutely love this tune; it ranks among the best tracks on *SLOB* for me. The spiralling acoustic guitar, mandolin, flute, and accordion all propel the tune forward, while Ian's delicate, understated singing and James Duncan's solid drumming create a perfect backdrop. At 1:34 minutes, a syncopated riff kicks in that cries out for a crunchy electric guitar. Where's Martin Barre when you need him? Ian solos over the top with breathy, trilling flute, reminiscent of the old days before he adopted the more formal style of playing the "heavy metal instrument" that was more classically Galwayesque The track returns to the main theme for the final verse, and then it's time to head home and listen to some more bird trilling in the next song.

Score 16/20

The Secret Language Of Birds Pt 2

On Jethro Tull's *Under Wraps* album, the title track is presented twice — once in an electric version and once acoustically — but both versions are essentially the same song, with the same chords and lyrics. However, in *SLOB*, the song and *SLOB* Pt 2 are completely different in terms of both music and lyrics, which is a clever and almost unique idea from Ian.

There are, of course, the songs "Wondering Aloud" and "Wandering Again" from early seventies Jethro Tull, where the second song is longer and incorporates some musical elements from the first, but with entirely different lyrics. So, while the two "Wandering" songs are similar, they are still distinct. In contrast, *SLOB* the song and *SLOB* Pt 2 are far more divergent. The *Pt 2* version is, perhaps, the most complex both lyrically and musically, and it is certainly to my personal taste.

The track references "A Nightingale In Berkeley Square," a song by Vera Lynn from 1940. The music was composed by Manning Sherwin, while the evocative, romantic lyrics were written by Eric Maschwitz — although he borrowed them from a short story titled *When The Nightingale Sang In Berkeley Square*, written by Michael Arlen in 1923.

Ian cleverly incorporates the nightingale theme into his lyrics, which is now twice removed from its original creators. If this were a 2025 pop song, the writing credits might read Anderson / Arlen / Lynn / Maschwitz / Sherwin, with remixing by DJ Giddings. But what about the nightingale itself? Surely the bird deserves a small royalty in bird seed for providing the inspiration, especially since it's unlikely to be found in central London, as nightingales typically prefer rural habitats.

I've been putting off looking at the lyrics, as they seem a bit tricky! I think it's a romantic song, but the writer seems to desire a relationship where his muse speaks to him in "bird song" as a means of achieving a deeper, more enlightened understanding. "Let's talk the secret language of birds" is a chat-up line I never tried, but perhaps I should have — it certainly worked for Ian. There are references to Hardy, a cheeky semaphore, and an Anderson-style train metaphor, all of which are very entertaining. "You with me?" says Ian in the sleeve notes regarding his lyrics. Not sure, Ian, but where would we be without those enigmatic, weirdly Andersonesque lyrics to keep us guessing and entertained?

Musically, the track is lively, with acoustic guitar, flute, and accordion interludes, all propelled by Darren Mooney's steady 4/4 drumming, which gives it an almost rock-like feel. If this track had been power-chorded and riffed up by Martin Barre's electric guitar, it could have made a great, eyeball-popping rock track on a Jethro Tull album. As it stands, it's still a great tune, one of the best on *SLOB*.

Score 14/20

Boris Dancing

This track could be referencing either Boris Johnson, Boris Yeltsin, or perhaps another Boris — the type of uncle everyone enjoys seeing at Christmas, but only for a few hours. Both Boris 1 and Boris 2 led their countries with what some might describe as flair and panache, while others might see it as a devil-may-care flippancy. Perhaps both started with good intentions, but as their baser instincts took over, they eventually found themselves "dancing for their suppers" as their popularity dwindled.

Since "Boris Dancing" was written in 1998 and released in 2000, we can reasonably assume that Ian is referencing Boris Yeltsin, who was known for his fondness for drink and dance during his time ruling Russia in his spare time, between 1991 and 1999.

Ian confirms this in his sleeve notes. The famous incident when Yeltsin danced at a political rally in Moscow's Red Square is well-documented and available on YouTube — he's in time, then out of time, and very much enjoying himself. Fortunately for us, he wasn't dancing while holding the nuclear button, or else Armageddon might have followed, and this delightful instrumental from Ian would never have seen the light of day.

Flute and accordion dominate the track, giving it a Russian jig with an Eastern flavour — something Tchaikovsky might have been proud of. Suddenly, the backing thickens, becoming more muscular, as none other than Jethro Tull's guitar hero Martin Barre strums away on a slightly amplified electric guitar. Ian and Andrew must have had fun with the percussion, as no one else is credited.

Does "Boris Dancing" attempt to mirror Yeltsin's dance moves in the YouTube clip? Well, sort of — it's a jaunty, lively, foot-tapping track that I thoroughly enjoyed hearing live at Jethro Tull gigs in the early 2000s.

Score 13/20

Circular Breathing

Circular breathing is a respiratory technique used by flute players and other wind instrument musicians to inhale through the nose while simultaneously exhaling through the mouth. It involves taking a deep breath and then storing air in the cheeks, slowly deflating them to produce a long, continuous exhale. This technique allows for extended notes, making it ideal for musicians who prefer a leisurely pace.

For example, famous saxophonist Kenny G once held an E flat note for over 45 minutes with the sax on a slow afternoon, setting a world record then, using circular breathing. This Kenny G duration is roughly the same as the length of Jethro Tull's *Thick as a Brick*, during which Ian Anderson plays about 555 intermittent flute notes (give or take, aproximately!), probably without using circular breathing.

I've taken a bit of poetic licence with these comparisons, despite trillingly counting the flute notes in and out. My more musically knowledgeable wife has informed me that circular breathing isn't necessary for playing the flute, but it can certainly help on occasion. Does Ian reference these lengthy musical techniques in the lyrics? Absolutely not!

Meanwhile, Constable and Lowry make an appearance in Ian's typically enigmatic lyrics. In the first verse, Ian imagines himself as a bird, searching for his love interest in Constable country, over the Stour Valley on the Essex/Suffolk border, near Flatford Mill — perhaps the scene of Mr. Constable's most famous painting, The Haywain.

In the second verse, he becomes a kite, looking down and reflecting on a row with his romantic muse. In the brief third verse of just three lines, Ian soars above a Manchester landscape, evoking the matchstick figures of Lowry and the imagery from Status Quo's "Pictures Of Matchstick Men" (as pointed out in the sleeve notes). All the while, the writer listens intently to the spiralling sounds of circular breathing.

As with many of Ian's lyrics, I don't always fully grasp the meaning, but they create a visual and aural experience for the listener's imagination. I particularly enjoy how the song transports me from Suffolk to Manchester in just 3.45 minutes.

The song begins with a clear, crisp acoustic guitar, accompanied by conga percussion and bass guitar. The three-line versette is repeated twice, featuring one of those signature Ian Anderson melodies that I've come to love in his songs with Jethro Tull. There's a touch of flute and lead acoustic guitar weaving in and out. While "Circular Breathing" may not be outstanding at first listen, it's an underrated gem that improves with repeated play.

Score 13/20

The Stormont Shuffle

In 1998, when this instrumental track was written, the Northern Ireland peace process was at a delicate stage of negotiation and debate. The seat of self-government for the province was Stormont Castle in East Belfast, where politicians from both the Catholic and Protestant communities would "shuttle" — or perhaps even "shuffle" — in and out, both physically and politically, as they navigated the peace talks.

On 10th April 1998, the Good Friday Agreement came into effect, ushering in a period of peace that, despite some challenges, has endured and remains in place today.

In this context, Ian Anderson crafted a bi-polar instrumental, split into two distinct parts, initially written separately to represent the Nationalist Protestant tradition and the Republican Catholic tradition.

While these two musical strains are different, they are also similar enough to coexist within the same three-minute piece. One might even wonder if you could remix the two strands to be played simultaneously without hearing the join. This musical technique symbolises the coming together of two religious and cultural identities that were once far apart but have now united, much like the two communities in the Good Friday Agreement.

While Ian Anderson may not be directly responsible for the peace process (with Tony Blair taking much of the credit), his musical insight is impressive, and he's certainly is a clever so and so pacifier! Perhaps Ian could write a tune to bring together Ukraine and Russia, or Israel and Palestine? Sadly, if only it were that simple.

The tune features flute and accordion at the forefront, underpinned by a drone and drums (possibly a bodhrán) to evoke an Irish jig flavour. After about two minutes, the second theme subtly begins to emerge. This new melody carries a warmth and jauntiness that the earlier theme lacked, hinting at the optimism and hope that the peace agreement would bring. It serves as a musical note of optimism to close *SLOB* on, leaving us with a sense of reconciliation and potential for the future.

Score 14/20

***

Like *Walk into Light* and *Divinities: Twelve Dances With God*, it has been an absolute pleasure to revisit *SLOB* in detail after so many years. Lyrically, it presents the usual challenges for my full understanding, yet I continue to appreciate Ian's ability to craft evocative, geographically anchored images with his words. As I listen, I find myself imagining landscapes, seascapes, and even "volcanoscapes." The lyrics conjure a sense of vivid Technicolor, particularly with Ian's references to painting in both the words and sleeve notes. In short, I feel the lyrics here represent a step up from *Walk Into Light*, where they sometimes felt a little lazy, complacent, and predictable.

My favourite tracks are "Montserrat," "Sanctuary," "The Jasmine Corridor," "Panama Freighter," and "SLOB Pt 2" (the song). However, the standout for me — perhaps for Ian too, and likely many fans — is "The Habanero Reel" for its fantastic tune, entertaining lyrics, and its seamless adaptation to live performances.

At this point, it's worth taking a moment to pay tribute to Mr Andrew Giddings, whose significant contributions to *Divinities* and *SLOB* cannot be overstated. His exceptional versatility as a musician, arranger, and confidant is evident in his ability to work across both classical flute albums and singer-songwriter albums with equal skill, leaving a lasting mark on these two records.

Looking ahead, it will be interesting to compare *SLOB* with *Rupi's Dance*, which is up next. While it may seem like another mainly acoustic Ian Anderson album, it ultimately turned out to be quite different in reality.

4
Rupi's Dance

Rupi's Dance serves as a duology natural companion piece to *SLOB*, offering another collection of acoustic-based music enhanced by flute embellishments, released just three years later in 2003. However, beyond this surface similarity, the differences between the two albums are quite pronounced.

Up to this point, Ian Anderson had relied heavily on the support of virtuoso keyboard players with exceptional arranging skills for his first three solo albums: Peter-John Vettese on *Walk Into Light*, and Andrew Giddings on both *Divinities: Twelve Dances with God* and *The Secret Language Of Birds*. In *Rupi's Dance*, the supporting cast is broader and more diverse, with only a few contributors directly connected to Jethro Tull.

Lyrically, the scope of *Rupi's Dance* is much wider than that of *The Secret Language Of Birds*. The earlier album was united by themes of geography and painting, whereas here Ian explores a variety of unrelated topics, delivering his characteristically enigmatic and meaningfully obtuse lyrics about whatever caught his attention at the time. The result is a collection of stand-alone tracks covering subjects as diverse as working with orchestras, romantic holidays, and a CNN TV presenter who is "musically well scanned."

Additionally, the album features two quintessential Anderson songs about cats, though the feline protagonists are of very different ages, at the start and end of life. This lack of thematic unity contrasts with Ian's later return to cohesive conceptual writing in *Thick As A Brick 2* in 2012 — but that's in the next chapter. Notably, *Rupi's Dance* also includes more electric guitar, played not by Martin Barre but by other contributors — a "funny old thing," indeed, for an Ian Anderson album.

By 2003, Ian was living a kind of musical dual life. On the one hand, he continued performing amplified, bombastic shows with Jethro Tull; on the other, he embarked on more intimate solo tours under the banner of *Rubbing Elbows*.

These solo tours were a mix of music and conversation: Ian would invite a local radio personality to interview him about his work with Tull and his solo material, interspersed with performances featuring at first playing along to backing tracks and then being accompanied by a small backing band. This group typically included Kit Morgan on guitars, Ian's son James Duncan on drums, and future Jethro Tull members David Goodier on bass and John O'Hara on keyboards and accordion. At the same time, Ian also embraced his role as a "rock god" during Tull performances, creating a curious artistic dichotomy.

Ian's decision to scale things down with *The Secret Language Of Birds* and *Rupi's Dance* rather than release them under the Jethro Tull name marked an intriguing shift in his career. Here on "*Rupi's Dance*" in particular he was determined to be a "one man band" all be it using others as session musicians rather than collaborators in the way Peter and Andrew were over the first three solo albums. Songs from *Rupi's Dance* were heavily featured on the *Rubbing Elbows* tours, where they translated well to a live setting (more on this later). Ultimately, *Rupi's Dance* is a distinctive album, showcasing Ian's desire to explore new almost random lyrical topics while continuing to captivate his audience.

The album features 13 tracks, with German-Hungarian musician Leslie Mandoki making the most frequent guest appearances, contributing drums and percussion on seven of them. Mandoki, whose background is in jazz rock, fled Hungary for Germany during the 1980s due to conflicts with the communist regime. In 1993, he formed the band Mandoki Soulmates, which released one album featuring Ian Anderson as a guest, thereby establishing their musical connection.

Laszlo Bencker, Mandoki's keyboard player, appears on six tracks, while The Sturcz String Quartet adds their effective string work to three. They were Gabor Csonka on 1st violin, Peter Szilagyi on 2nd violin, Gyula Benko on viola and Andras

Sturcz on cello. They also provided the sympathetic strings on the wonderful "First Snow On Brooklyn" from *The JethroTull Christmas Album,* also out in 2003. Beyond these contributors, various other musicians make appearances on a track-by-track basis, details of which I will highlight as I review each song. Notably, Andrew Giddings — long-time Tull keyboard player and key collaborator on previous solo albums — features sparingly, providing bass and keyboards on just two tracks, including "Not Ralitsa Vassileva."

Naturally, Ian Anderson is present on all tracks, handling vocals, acoustic guitar, flute, piccolo, mandolin, percussion, bass, and accordion, all while balancing on one leg and feeding his cats. Is there anything the man can't do?

Speaking of cats, "Rupi," the young kitty feline inspiration for the album title, makes a cameo appearance on the album sleeve, photographed alongside Ian by his son, James Duncan. "Rupi" playfully mimics Ian's iconic one-legged flute-playing pose. Ian's extensive sleeve notes accompany the packaging, each infused with his trademark "funny old" musings, which might just give "funny old" listeners like me a fighting chance at grasping the meaning behind 11 of the 13 tracks — two being instrumentals. Let's find out!

***

Calliandra Shade (The Cappuccino Song)

Calliandra is a genus of flowering plants belonging to the pea family. These versatile plants can take the form of shrubs, small plants, or even trees up to 20 feet tall — just enough to provide shade for a sunlit outdoor café.

However, unless you live in the tropics or frequent a café within a greenhouse like the Eden Project, you're unlikely to encounter a Calliandra tree in your town. While it is possible to grow Calliandra in the UK, the climate is not warm enough for it to flourish as a tree — at least not yet.

Global warming may change that in the future, though it offers little else to look forward to. Interestingly, while you cannot brew coffee from Calliandra, you *can* make a type of tea from its bark, as is done in Peru. In the context of the song "Calliandra Shade," however, the reference is literal — depicting the shade of a tree as a retreat for a voyeur, coffee drinker, or wordsmith.

Cappuccino, a globally beloved steamed milk coffee, serves as the perfect excuse for café-goers to while away hours watching the world go by. Ian's lyrics vividly capture such observational moments, referencing locals, ragamuffin children, lame dogs, and cats. His sleeve notes accompanying the song are equally entertaining — particularly if you read them quickly. Ian's description of frothy coffee is... well, let's just say it wouldn't pass the test of decorum in 2025. Sad man that I am though, I am still laughing. No, I won't quote the sleeve notes verbatim — you will have to beg steal or borrow the CD.

Musically, Ian handles all instrumentation apart from the drums, which are provided by his son, James Duncan. Acoustic guitar, bass, standard flute, and a slightly slurring wooden flute are layered to create a rich and evocative introduction.

Ian's vocals are as effective as they were three years ago on *The Secret Language Of Birds*, carrying a subtle melancholy that contrasts with the upbeat nature of the music itself. At over six minutes, the track does feel a little long, but it's more than half good — and certainly not half bad. Better things lie ahead!

Score 11/20

Rupi's Dance

Songs about cats of the "cool" variety — those cannabis-smoking, jazz-loving, hip young movers and shakers of a bygone age, who threw up an arty alternative lifestyle — are plentiful. However, songs that delve into the life and times of an actual domesticated feline are far rarer. In fact, two artists come to mind: Ian Anderson and... a little rock group by the name of Jethro Tull. Surely there's a connection there, somewhere?

Why not write a song expressing love, devotion, and attention to a newborn kitty, just 14 weeks old? Ian Anderson, a self-confessed cat lover, does precisely that, crafting poetic lyrics for his charming young cute feline princess. And that's the essence of "Rupi's Dance" — a sweet, straightforward song with no hidden meaning or layers of enigmatic wordsmithery. Rupi, the dancing moggy, even lends her name to the album itself.

As an album title, *Rupi's Dance* feels refreshingly simple and unpretentious — perhaps even a "funny old title." It's not a grand concept like *The Secret Language Of Birds* or *Divinities: Twelve Dances with God*. It doesn't suggest a thematic journey, as *Thick As A Brick 2* or *Homo Erraticus* might, nor does it imply a voyage toward utopia like *Walk Into Light*. The title could be viewed as either a "cop-out" or a stroke of artistic simplicity. Did Ian finish recording the songs and then pick one to name the album? Or was the title pre-planned? Answers on a "Postcard Day," please, Ian.

Musically, this track features Ian on flute and guitar, with David Goodier contributing a touch of stand-up bass that enhances the overall feel. It's a charming and enjoyable piece, though the following track takes things up another notch.

Score 12/20

Lost In Crowds

This track is a deeply introspective, self-analytical piece — an "I" song filled with self-reproach, which is quite uncharacteristic of Ian Anderson. Here, he almost channels John Lennon, baring his soul in a way that feels unusually vulnerable. Gone are the small talk and starry parties; instead, we're told to get "lost in crowds," keep our heads down below the parapet, watch the world go by and transform the experience into musical song. Ian's sentiments in the second verse feel relatable, particularly for those like me who've endured the awkward social pressures of house parties, attempting to engage in witty small talk while nervously queuing for the only available toilet.

Instrumentally, the track balances light and shade, delicacy and bombast, acoustic interludes and rock-out moments. The weaving of these elements results in a strong, dynamic tune — arguably the best so far on the album.

Lyrically, there are some fascinating touches. For instance, "blether" in the second line of the second verse is a Scottish term meaning "to talk in a long-winded way without much substance." This could easily describe a significant portion of classic prog rock lyrics from the 1970s. However, it doesn't apply to Ian Anderson, whose masterful works like *Thick As A Brick* and *A Passion Play* always made perfect sense to me — well, most of the time.

The term might better fit Jon Anderson of Yes fame, whose *Tales From Topographic Oceans* epitomised lyrical "blethering" of epic proportions. In this track, however, Ian's use of "blether" feels self-deprecating, aligning with the song's overall tone of vulnerability. This introspective approach reveals a charming and endearing side to Ian's lyricism.

Musically, the core ensemble of Ian, Leslie Mandoki, Laszlo Bencker, and The Sturcz String Quartet is joined by two punchy guitarists, Ossi Schaller and George Kopecsni, whose power chords amplify the track's darker moments. Ian's melody shines with its melancholic undertones, complemented by his "older," more delicate vocals, which add depth and poignancy. The instrumental break is a standout moment, where piano, flute, and strings interweave seamlessly, evoking memories of "Part Of The Machine" from Jethro Tull's *Crest Of A Knave* box set.

The final verse, referencing the *Herald Tribune*, builds to an emotional climax with violin harmonies and tenderly sad vocals, creating a powerful yet sensitively soothing effect. It's a standout track that sets a high bar for the album.

But then, the next track might just surpass it—funny old thing, this album!

Score 14/20

A Raft Of Penguins

It's likely that Ian Anderson chose this title because a penguin's sleek, tuxedo-like appearance resembles the formal attire of male orchestral players, all neatly arranged on the "raft" of the concert floor. Perhaps. Either way, Ian's sleeve notes for this track are longer than the lyrics themselves and provide an entertaining account of the stylistic clash between his improvisational, "flutey on the hoof" tendencies and the disciplined, formally trained classical musicians who reliably play all the notes in the correct order — regardless of whether it's a good day or a bad one.

In the early 2000s, Ian's core solo band consisted of John O'Hara on keyboards, David Goodier on bass, James Duncan on drums, and new addition Florian Opahle on guitar. This group toured with local orchestras, performing rearranged Jethro Tull classics and more faithful renditions of Ian's solo material.

Acting as a bridge between Ian and the orchestra was often John O'Hara, whose ability to read sheet music like a book, contrasted with Ian's more instinctive approach. Ian, of course, brought something unique to the table with his off-the-cuff, double-tonguing, mean, dirty virtuosity on the flute, embodying the tension between rock star spontaneity and orchestral precision.

Despite Ian's "affectionate musings" about leading an orchestra, the collaboration worked splendidly. A clear demonstration of this success is the 2005 DVD release *Ian Anderson Plays The Orchestral Jethro Tull,* where Ian performs with the Neue Philharmonie Frankfurt. Even the classical players appear to embrace the spirit of the music, with a touch of syncopated head-banging during the grand "Locomotive Breath" finale. In the end, everything came together brilliantly.

Musically, this track is a soaring triumph. The harmony between flute and piccolo, combined with the energetic strings of The Sturcz String Quartet, creates an exhilarating melody that simply soars some more. Ian's vocals are impassioned, brimming with conviction, and there's even a nod to "The Whistler" (a classic from *Songs From The Wood*). This song is an absolute powerhouse — one of the standout tracks of the album and an undeniable delight!

Score 17/20

A Week Of Moments

Funny events, holidays, especially in the UK, which often come with unpredictable weather, leaving much to be desired. For my wife and I it's typically a single week in June spent dodging wind and rain in Devon. Still, these trips are made worthwhile by indulging in some romantic "Passion Play." Ian Anderson's lyrics, however, take the concept of a romantic getaway to another level.

In "A Week Of Moments," a "Passion Play" stretches across "ten thousand minutes," which equates to 166 hours — or roughly seven days. While it's safe to assume Ian is speaking figuratively, if taken literally, such a feat might require a liberal application of pharmaceutical assistance to keep it up (oh dear!) over the whole week.

Ian's lyrics also include mentions of wine, sunshine, photographs, and a pool, indicating that this idealised holiday isn't entirely about indulgent decadence. The title, "A Week Of Moments," perfectly encapsulates a nostalgic look back at treasured memories: the "Do you remember when we... and then you... Oh yes, you did" kind of reminiscing that makes you eager to do it all over again the following year — albeit perhaps with slightly less of the "Passion Play."

Musically, the track follows the typical structure of an Ian Anderson acoustic song, but there's a delightful addition of a repeated triangle sound that pops up throughout, lending a subtle charm. The melody is pleasant, though somewhat sombre, and Ian's vocals carry a world-weary tone, as if he's yearning for home with a good book instead of an action-packed holiday. However, the mood lifts with a wonderfully breathy, trilling flute solo, injecting a burst of vitality before the song returns to its original tone — only for the flute to make a triumphant reappearance at the end.

This song is an enigma. On the one hand, it feels too gloomy to capture the joy of a romantic holiday; on the other, the flute solos are absolutely brilliant. Perhaps they symbolise the intense, passionate moments of the getaway, or maybe they simply stand as exquisite musical interludes. Either way, it's those instrumental flourishes that elevate "A Week Of Moments" and make it memorable.

Score 10/20

A Hand Of Thumbs

It is extremely rare — occurring in approximately 1 in 100 births — for a baby to be born with an extra thumb, a condition noted to be more common among Asian American boys. However, a hand of thumbs is, from my admittedly limited research, a physical impossibility. So, what exactly could Ian Anderson be referring to here?

As usual, the answer lies in his ever-enlightening sleeve notes, offering clarity for those "thick as a brick" (or "two short planks") like me. Perhaps Ian could have called this track "Sweaty Palm Syndrome," reflecting the implied nervous encounter with a "seductive stranger" that ends in clumsy failure.

Alternatively, "All Fingers And Thumbs" might have captured the essence of his character's fumbling awkwardness, as he figuratively "drops the handshake" in a mix of trepidation and self-doubt. But instead, Ian landed on "A Hand Of Thumbs," which, while enigmatic, stands as a brilliantly original title. Of course, one suspects Ian is "role-playing" here, narrating the misadventures of some other shy, silly so and so — and certainly not himself... right?

Musically, this track shares a punchy, rock-driven feel with "Lost In Crowds," thanks in large part to the guitars of Ossi Schaller and George Kopecsni. It also features the recording debut of David Goodier, who would go on to become a long-standing collaborator with Ian and Jethro Tull, here playing bass and double bass.

The instrumentation effectively conveys a sense of nervous tension, trembling with apprehension, before the full ensemble kicks in with a power-packed, almost metallic energy. By the end, the track escalates to a powerful climax, where crunching metal-style guitar chords are complemented by a bold, "heavy metal instrument" flute solo — an unexpected but thrilling outro.

Despite all the musical bravado, it seems Ian's protagonist doesn't quite win over the girl by the final trill of the song. Nonetheless, "A Hand Of Thumbs" closes with an exhilarating flourish, leaving the listener on a high even if the story ends with a touch of bittersweet irony.

Score 12/20

Eurology

This track contains no lyrics, which might seem to simplify matters, but Ian's characteristically amusing sleeve notes suggest there's still room for a playful double entendre. As it's an "-ology," it must logically involve the study of something — be it European affairs or, as hinted, urological issues. Perhaps the energetic and vibrant tune reflects the plight of an elderly European gentleman in urgent need of a toilet, because in their withered old age, they are "prostratingly" challenged by an enlarged "one," leading to peeing problems. Or perhaps it's just a bouncy, foot-tapping instrumental that invites listeners to join in with a cheerful "la la" accompaniment.

The track marks the recording debut of John O'Hara, another future mainstay in Ian's and Jethro Tull's line-up. Another in the band's tradition of virtuoso musicians, John likely earned his place for his skilful use of the "squeezy thing" accordion, which he plays to great effect here. David Goodier on bass and Leslie Mandoki on drums round out the ensemble, delivering a tightly coordinated performance.

Musically, the piece is jaunty, lively, and bursting with a jig-like energy. It's packed with the hallmarks of a classic Ian Anderson instrumental, save perhaps for the absence of a metal monster, roaring Martin Barre guitar solo. John and Ian trade deft mini-solos throughout, backed by the pulsating rhythm provided by David and Leslie. A delightful flourish comes at the track's close with a whimsical bass loop from David, adding to its charm.

For me, this is a standout instrumental, brimming with energy and fun. It's also a track Ian and Jethro Tull occasionally performed live to great effect. And if we old codgers do find ourselves needing a toilet break, the song's brief 3:14 runtime ensures you won't be kept waiting too long!

Score 14/20

Old Black Cat

This is another cat song to join those already in the Tull repertoire (such as "...And The Mouse Police Never Sleep" and "Hunt By Numbers"), as well as a companion piece to the earlier track "Rupi's Dance" on this album. However, while "Rupi" is a youthful, lively cat, "Old Black Cat" reflects a very different stage of life, serving as a poignant farewell to a beloved family pet. Whether sentimental or not, this track is undoubtedly a tender tribute.

Lyrically, the "Old Black Cat" seems to have led a routine and unremarkable life as a family moggy, unaware that he would be immortalised in song upon his death. He passed away just before Christmas, prompting Ian to compose a gentle, plaintive ode, as one might do when mourning a loved one.

Musically, Ian primarily performs solo on this track, with guitars and flutes, although David Goodier adds a subtle touch with double bass. The chord progression and melody strike a delicate balance, capturing both the joy of fond memories and the sorrow of recent loss. How does Ian Anderson manage to convey such a complex emotion with so little? Acoustic guitar, vocals, and interludes of flute are all it takes to create a song that resonates deeply with me.

And that, I believe, is the full extent of Ian's cat-themed compositions in the universe of IA and JT. I, for one, am simply grateful that Ian wasn't a fan of goldfish!

Score 15/20

Photo Shop

Another everyday, relatable song from Ian, this time about the awkward world of poorly timed and poorly taken holiday snaps, captured in all their embarrassing glory — including "topless wives" to be reviewed by the film developer. This was written before photography became so personal, with mobile phone snaps printed at home in 2025.

On *Rupi's Dance*, the theme seems to be "no theme," with a desire to be as varied as possible in the subject matter. Ian has the remarkable ability to write a song about virtually anything and everything, yet somehow, in his unique Andersonesque style, make it work lyrically.

There are no heavy, prog fantastic rock lyrics here, though plenty of clever wordplay. As always, I'm partial to songs with a railway reference — even a tenuous one, and in this case, Paddington Station gets a mention. Of course, the lyrics would evolve drastically in Ian's subsequent solo albums, leading me back to frowning and deep contemplation as I try to interpret the work of Ian, the prog wordsmith.

Ian plays everything on this track, including the accordion, since presumably John O'Hara or Andrew Giddings were unavailable. The melody is one of Ian's lighter, quirky tunes, wandering along at a moderate pace, with vocals interrupted by flute interjections.

Around the two-minute mark, there's a flute solo that seems to cry out for some grand, metal-style backing — perhaps from the missing Martin Barre. Overall, it's a pleasant enough tune, but quite middling within the context of the album. Surely the next track will be better — and, gosh, indeed, it most certainly is!

Score 11/20

Pigeon Flying Over Berlin Zoo

As with much of *Rupi's Dance*, the sleeve notes are often just as intriguing and insightful as the lyrics themselves. Ian recounts a visit to Berlin Zoo one mid-morning during a tour, where he observes a pigeon in the sky, taking in a bird's-eye view of the enclosed animals below. Inspired, he writes a song about it in his head, remembers the melody, and records it instantly back at the hotel on a mini disc. Remarkable, but then again, if you're Ian Anderson, the writing muse can strike at any time, in any place. This perfectly captures the spontaneous nature of his creative process, as explained in the matter-of-fact sleeve notes titled "I Just Popped Out to the Zoo."

The pigeon's lofty vantage point at Berlin Zoo provides a fitting perspective, with lyrics that are straightforward (at least for me) but still laced with Ian's characteristic wordplay. The use of "Pigeon English" and "pigeon-toed" in verse two works particularly well, and it's easy to see why Ian chose a pigeon as his aerial observer — using a sparrow or even a wandering (over Germany) albatross might not have offered the same clever wordplay.

Musically, the track just takes off, just like a bird — of course it does! It features the full band ensemble, with Ian, David Goodier, Leslie Mandoki, Laszlo Bencker, and The Sturcz String Quartet, along with James Duncan on drums and Andrew Giddings on additional keyboards (so far avoiding overlapping with future Tull keyboardist John O'Hara).

The song features a brilliant chord and melody progression, with Ian's flute reprising the vocal melody around the two-minute mark in a way that's simply outstanding. The track swells and swings in equal measure, particularly around the "think about it" lyrical motif. This is yet another song that would have made a fantastic Jethro Tull track, especially with some soaring electric guitar — Martin Barre, you can come back from lunch now!

Score 16/20

Griminelli's Lament

This piece is so lyrically understated that it doesn't have any lyrics at all. Instead, it's a beautiful, classically themed instrumental dedicated to Ian's Italian flautist friend, Andrea Griminelli. Andrea had recently gone through a break-up from his girl friend, and Ian wrote this lament for him, featuring two flutes, in an effort to lift his spirits. Interestingly, Ian didn't invite Andrea to play the second flute on the recording — a decision that may have been for the best, as Andrea might have become even more despondent and suicidal, leaving him unable to later perform the piece with Ian live on several occasions.

The track features just Ian, David Goodier, and John O'Hara, and it conveys a deep sense of sadness, with its lilting melody carried by two counterpoint flutes. The playing has a folky, Celtic quality to it, and my wife, Linda, who is classically trained, suggested that a real harpsichord in the background might have enhanced the piece further — and I have to agree. Ian could have easily carved out a second career composing break-up instrumentals to cheer people up.

I've managed to not break up with my wife during the "lament" and have kept my sanity intact, despite the lack of harpsichord while listening to this track. It's cool, quaint, and melancholy, but the next song — well, just ask Ralitsa, because it's something truly special.

Score 13/20

Not Ralitsa Vassileva

Ralitsa Vassileva, a Bulgarian, is currently, in 2025, a lecturer in journalism at the Grady College of Journalism and Mass Communication in the USA. When Ian Anderson first "knew" her, she was a prominent anchor-woman at CNN Television News. If Ian had wanted to write a song about a newsreader, he could have chosen an English male or female — but that would have missed the point. The real magic in this song lies in the clever rhyme of "Ralitsa Vassileva" with "CNN in America," which I absolutely love. So did the real Ralitsa, who got to meet and even sing with Ian during her own song on The Rubbing Elbow Tours.

The lyrics describe a dinnertime conversation, where second-hand news is passed on through a slightly drunken mumble by a female companion who, it turns out, was "Not Ralitsa Vassileva." Ralitsa wasn't even present at the dinner, but she became immortalised in song in a way neither she nor we could have expected. She became, if not a hero to millions, at least a hero to me and to others who bought *Rupi's Dance*.

Musically, it's a full ensemble piece, with Andrew Giddings and John O'Hara likely competing to play the accordion — a battle John won, while Andrew played supplementary keyboards and bass guitar, both with great skill. It's also worth noting the role of Andrew Giddings, who served as musical director for *Divinities: Twelve Dances With God* and *The Secret Language Of Birds*. It must have been difficult for him on *Rupi's Dance*, given his reduced non collaborator role.

The music swings with a 6/8 time signature, as my waltz-loving wife, Linda, informs me. After a quick intro, the music bubbles along effortlessly, but the highlights are the lines "Not Ralitsa Vassileva" and "a long way from here to CNN in America," which feature a quintessential Ian Anderson melody to die for. The singing is interrupted by a flute cadenza that follows the vocal melody, and it sounds just wonderful. As I write these words, my karaoke rendition of this track might almost be enough to make Ian and Ralitsa proud... but not quite!

Score 17/20

Two Short Planks

When I was a lad growing up in Nottingham, it was common for friends to affectionately call someone "thick as two short planks" or simply "thick as a br...", or something along those lines. This must be Ian Anderson's companion song to *Thick As A Brick*, where "two short planks" replace the "brick" in a similar vein. The same colloquial expressions would have been used where Ian grew up in Blackpool, too. However, unlike *Thick As A Brick*, which was a 43-minute prog rock epic with deep musings on the human condition, "Two Short Planks" is a much shorter and lighter piece.

The song humorously reflects Ian's self-deprecating view of his academic abilities, particularly in subjects like maths and science, where he considered himself "thick as two short planks." However, I doubt his teachers shared that view. Clever pupil Anderson did his exams early and went on to have a successful career as an erudite, intelligent rock star, able to produce great songs with both lyrical and musical substance. Not bad for someone who thought of himself as a "two short planks" kind of person!

Musically, the song is brilliant and a perfect way to end the album. It's mostly a solo Ian performance, with some bass help from David Goodier. The tune is jaunty, playful, and surprisingly cheerful, given the academic incompetence it's poking fun at. But it's all tongue-in-cheek, and the mood is light-hearted. After all, Ian did pretty well in the end!

Score 15/20

***

And that's the end of *Rupi's Dance*. I think it's a remarkable album. Overall, it features quality songs that are exceptionally well played and produced, with intriguing lyrics and beautiful melodies. No topic, no matter how trivial or global, was too insignificant for an Ian Anderson song, and the album's broad, non-thematic subject matter could be seen as either a blessing or a curse — especially if you prefer albums with a cohesive concept. But for those of you who like your albums to be more eclectic, you'd get your wish in another nine years with *Thick As A Brick 2*.

Some of these tracks were played live, primarily by Ian during his *Rubbing Elbow* Tours, or with orchestras, such as on the *Neue Philharmonie Frankfurt* DVD mentioned earlier. "Eurology," "Calliandra Shade," and "Griminelli's Lament" all feature on this album. I have a vague recollection of hearing "Eurology" during a Tull tour somewhere. However, the most popular live track from Ian's first four solo albums has undoubtedly been "In The Grip Of Stronger Stuff" from *Divinities*. Quite rightly so — it's brilliant — and was performed frequently by both Ian and Tull for many years.

It was sometimes tricky keeping track of exactly who played on which track, as many of the musicians never contributed to another Ian Anderson or Jethro Tull album. Sadly, *Rupi's Dance* marked the final recording contribution of Andrew Giddings, who had been Ian's go-to musical arranger, idea man, and support for many years. His contribution to *Divinities* and *The Secret Language Of Birds* cannot be overstated. On the other hand, *Rupi's Dance* saw the introduction of John O'Hara and David Goodier, who continue to work with Ian and Tull to this day.

I can't help but think of *Rupi's Dance* as a companion piece to *The Secret Language Of Birds*. Both albums feature a collection of stand-alone songs. *The Secret Language Of Birds* has more of a sense of colour and warmth due to its painting references and geographical landscapes, while *Rupi's Dance* presents a fuller, denser sound with heavier instrumentation, which might give it more of a personal connection for me. Which is the better album? Right now, it's too close to call, but I suspect my thoughts will evolve by the time I reach my conclusion and tally up the scores.

My favourite tracks? There are so many, but "A Raft Of Penguins" and "Not Ralitsa Vassileva" are the standout gems. My least favourite? Well, I'll leave that for you to figure out.

And now, for something completely different — though it took another nine years to come to fruition. The next album? A funny old "brick"!

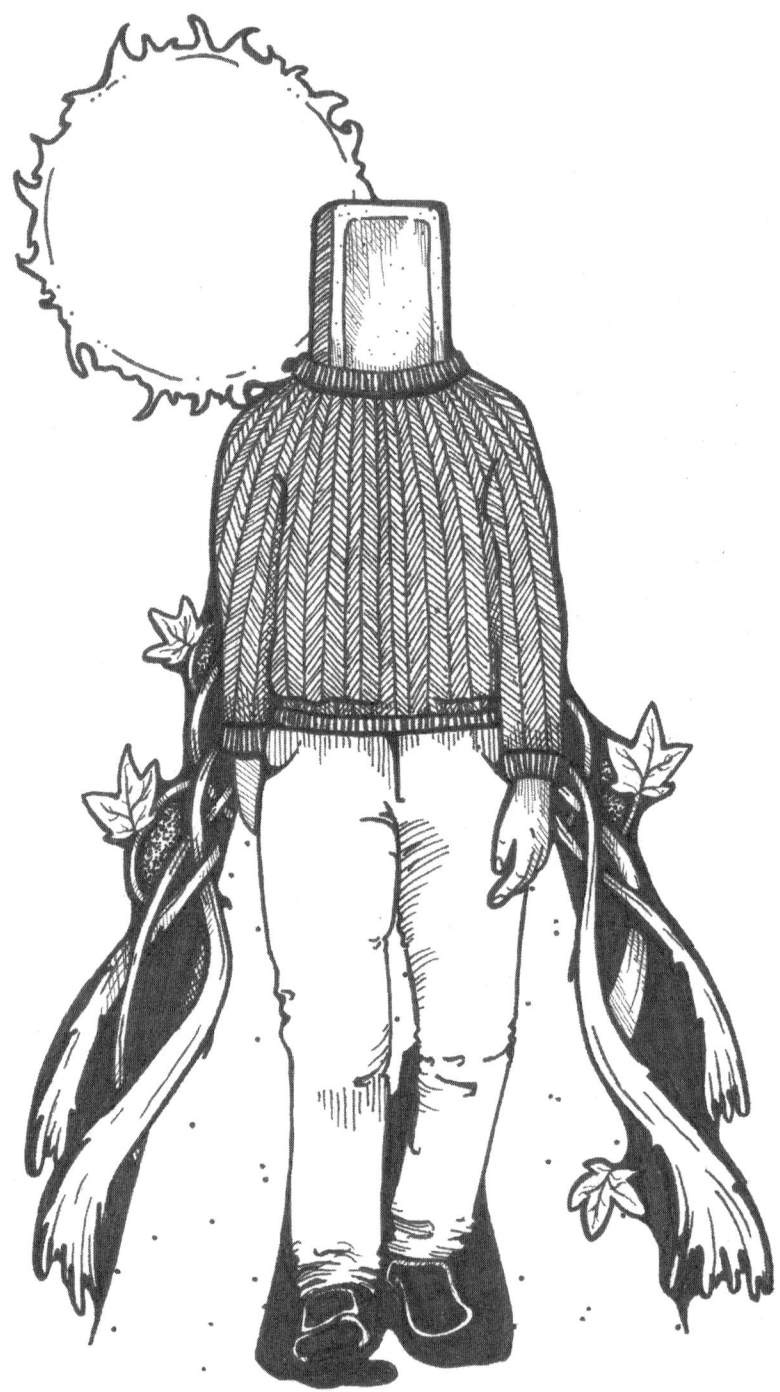

5
TAAB 2
(Thick As A Brick 2)

In 2012, the mysteriously vanished and somewhat dubious Gerald Bostock was 48 years old. However, it turns out that back in 1972, when he wrote the lyrics for *Thick As A Brick*, he and his parents had fibbed about his age. He wasn't 8, as they claimed, but in fact 10, which made him 50 in 2012.

By then, Ian Anderson had long lost contact with the aging Gerald and was left wondering what might have become of him over the years. What "what-ifs," maybes, and could-have-beens might have shaped Gerald's life and led him down his (un)chosen path? Had he become a monk in a Tibetan monastery, or perhaps a hedge fund manager making millions and retiring early to Spain? Ian decided to explore five different scenarios for Gerald and build *TAAB 2* around them. The best outcome, however, would be for Gerald to mysteriously remain absent, allowing Ian to continue messing with his alternative timeline for the album.

In my earlier book *Life Is A Long Song: A Compendium of Jethro Tull In 33 1/3 Songs*, I carried on the joke that Gerald Bostock was a real person, which I hope provided some entertainment. However, there's only so far you can take a joke before it risks crossing a line, and anyone named Gerald Bostock in real life might take umbrage.

So, I must categorically clarify: Gerald Bostock is not a real person (really), but rather a fictional creation of Ian Anderson's imagination. Sorry, Gerald — you've been exposed. So, while the opening paragraph might have had an element of truth, this is what really happened... or at least, maybe it is?

A quick history lesson is in order. *Thick As A Brick* was released in 1972, reaching No.1 on the US album charts and No.5 in the UK. In 2010 and 2011, there were suggestions that Jethro Tull should follow up the album. The most convincing suggestion came from Derek Shulman, former member of Gentle Giant, a respected musical peer and now a record company executive. By early 2011, Ian had given in with a resigned "all right then" and began planning the album. Gerald was to have five possible lives: banker, homeless man, military man, churchman (chorister), and the most ordinary man. The concept, theme, and lyrics would revolve around these scenarios, resulting in a 53-minute prog rock, concept album epic.

TAAB 2 was to be released 40 years after the original, with Ian being the only musician involved in both. Only Mike Oldfield, with *Tubular Bells 1, 2,* and *3*, and Meat Loaf, with *Bat Out of Hell 1, 2,* and *3*, had ever attempted anything similar. It was a significant risk for Ian, but perhaps the biggest gamble of all was releasing the album under his own name, not as Jethro Tull, and without the legendary Martin Barre playing on it. Would the album be any good? Only time would tell.

Throughout the 2000s, Ian's primary role remained with Jethro Tull, but his true passion seemed to lie in his solo live performances, whether on his own or with his band. Jethro Tull, rightly or wrongly, was perceived by observers — and by Ian himself — as a rock powerhouse, attracting enthusiastic, often drunken or stoned crowds, especially in the USA, who wanted the hits played loudly.

Ian, however, felt strongly that he no longer wanted to continue in this vein; he wanted his audience to listen attentively. In contrast, Ian's solo concerts were seen as quiet, dignified affairs, where fans came for the music rather than a raucous atmosphere. By 2011, Ian had grown weary of the Jethro Tull moniker and wished to perform under his own.

As for the Tull band members, John O'Hara (keyboards) and David Goodier (bass) were already part of Ian's solo band. Doane Perry, Tull's drummer since 1984, was unwell and needed time to recuperate in the USA during 2011, which allowed the new drummer, Scott Hammond, to join the fold for *TAAB 2*.

The biggest question, however, was about Martin Barre, the iconic Tull guitarist since 1969. Ian and Martin had several in-depth conversations during this period, and Ian says they agreed that Jethro Tull would go on hiatus for the foreseeable future, with Martin free to pursue other projects. Over the years, Martin has expressed disappointment about being "dropped" in such a manner. Meanwhile, Ian had been working on *TAAB 2* with the help of John O'Hara and solo band guitarist Florian Opahle, who was more than capable, having the licks and chops to play guitar, with exceptional skill. When it came time to record *TAAB 2* and tour the album, Florian was in the mix, and Martin was not.

This situation raised a significant issue for many fans and critics: How could *TAAB 2* exist without Martin Barre? I will revisit this point in my closing remarks for *TAAB 2*, but for now, suffice to say that Florian did a superb job, and as any football manager would, Ian Anderson is at liberty to choose who he wants to kick his footballs and play his music.

Alongside Ian, John, David, Scott, and Florian, Ryan O'Donnell contributed additional vocals, while Peter Judge played trumpet, flugelhorn, tenor horn, and E-flat tuba. The renowned Steven Wilson of Porcupine Tree, famous for his remastering of countless prog rock albums, handled the mixing. Ryan joined the core group for the subsequent live tour of both *TAAB 1* and *TAAB 2*, but more on that after I review the song tracks.

The album was recorded in late 2011 and released on 2nd April 2012. It came in another mock newspaper sleeve, this time designed to resemble an online journal called "www.StCleve.com."

Bogdan Zarkowski, who had previously worked on *Divinities* and *The Secret Language Of Birds*, once again contributed to the artwork. The stories featured the same kind of parochial localism as the 1972 *TAAB 1* newspaper, and I believe there was even an actual website called StCleve.com, where additional short stories for *TAAB 2* were published. Meanwhile, I will explore the album's chart positions, critical reviews, and live performances after discussing the song-by-song content.

Now, it's time for a song-by-song analysis of the seventeen

tracks, featuring some complex storytelling lyrics and tricky time signatures that are sure to leave me dumbfoundingly scratching my head. Wish me luck, as I try to make my way to break on through to the other side.

To begin, the structure of *TAAB 2* is fairly intricate, so here's a breakdown. The album consists of 2 units, 9 sections, and 13 songs, incorporating 4 melodies (according to the ever-reliable source that is most of the time, Wikipedia). If we leave out the medleys, this gives us 17 tracks in total, including one instrumental, which is how I'll approach it. The units and sections will be indicated in capitals as I go through. So, let's get started.

DIVERGENCE: Intervention, Parallel Possibilities

PEBBLES THROWN

From A Pebble Thrown

There are endless possibilities when a stone is tossed into a pond, symbolising a "birthing" moment that sends ripples and waves in all directions, shaping the course of a life. In verse one, our young hero, Gerald, takes a ghost train ride towards near oblivion but just manages to scrape through, finding his way onto an elevator in verse two, which then stops at every floor of life. Where should young Gerald get off? What would be the best choice? By verse three, the possibilities seem endless, but I wouldn't want to be in his shoes — it certainly seems like a grim start for poor, infantile Gerald.

Ian's lyrics here delve into heavy-duty, parallel worlds and alternate realities, where each waking moment or nightmare serves as a pinch point leading to a different possible outcome. I'm starting to suspect that *TAAB 2* is shaping up to be a dreaded, dastardly, seriously super concept album — which, of course, could turn out to be a lot of fun to try to wrap my head around!

Musically, the track opens with stiff, thudding chordal chops reminiscent of the closing moments of *TAAB 1*'s side one, lasting for about thirty seconds. Then, Ian's delicate yet crystal-clear vocals enter, eventually accompanied by the full band, playing what sounds unmistakably like proper rock music.

This is a real shock after the acoustic, minstrel-style music of *The Secret Language Of Birds* and *Rupi's Dance*. It's unmistakably Jethro Tull but also a million miles away from Ian's previous four solo albums.

This isn't a bad thing at all — just a surprise, in that typical Andersonesque "fooled you" fashion. It's very much a scene-setting song, both lyrically and musically, for the album to come, and it does its job perfectly.

The most famous pebble-themed song in prog rock circles is probably "Take A Pebble" by Emerson, Lake & Palmer, released in 1970. In it, Greg Lake sings of the "pebble" and the "ripples" disturbing the water of our lives, a similar "what if" effect to the one in our song.

Who would have thought that a single pebble tossed into water could have such far-reaching consequences for both Ian Anderson and ELP? Did the ELP song influence Ian? It seems highly unlikely. Keith Emerson's stunning piano playing in their version is very different, and both songs sound entirely distinct from one another.

Score 12/20

Pebbles Instrumental

The title feels a bit of a cop-out; perhaps "Pebble for Flute and Rock Band in a Major Key" would have been a more fitting choice. Nevertheless, it's not a bad little tune, and thankfully there are no lyrics to bewilder me this time.

The track features a circular melody, continually interrupted by the "Thick As A Brick" vocal refrain, with a charming flute solo at its heart. After that, everyone else takes their turn with solos. The song moves along smoothly in 4/4 time, making it foot-tappable and vaguely head-bangable, with a crunching, gutsy rock 'n' roll ending.

Score 10/20

Might-Have-Beens

And now, for something completely different — and that's no understatement! We are treated to a party political broadcast by the Pebble party. At just fifty seconds, it presents a series of pinch points and turning moments, exploring the multiple possible worlds and universes in which Gerald's life could unfold. Ian narrates the scenario options for Gerald in his clear, distinct speaking voice. In the final "what ifs," a little bird song (borrowed from *The Secret Language Of Birds*) accompanies the narration, but otherwise, it's just Ian throughout.

This track is an odd one, being entirely without music. As part of *TAAB 2* and its concept, it might make sense. However, I can never quite decide whether I like it or not, whether in the studio or live. Is it a cop-out, or a moment of great artistic clarity? I'll leave that for you to decide.

Score 8/20

GERALD THE BANKER

Upper Sixth Loan Shark

In this track, we see Gerald in his first scenario, where he earns his stripes as a financial wheeler-dealer while also being a typical sixth-former, ripping people off. All of this is covered in just over one minute and thirteen seconds of song. It serves as a lyrical warm-up for the epic track that follows.

The music is whimsically acoustic, featuring a lovely melody, with Ian's vocals clear and concise. This piece is essentially an overture, setting the stage for what's to come next.

Score 12/20

Banker Bets, Banker Wins

In my (ever so slightly biased) opinion, this is an absolute gem of a song — one of the top three tracks on the album, and it really rocks! It's foot-tappable and head-bangable, perfect for air flautists and air guitarists everywhere. The lyrics are great too.

By 2012, bankers — rhyming with... er... — had earned a

rather bad reputation following the 2008 financial collapse, and rightly so. Being a hedge fund manager at a bank seemed like a gilt-edged way to make a lot of money while betting on things going wrong. Then there were the banker bonuses, which infuriated the cash-strapped public. All of this is brilliantly captured in Ian's sharp and ironic lyrics. The only other song that comes close in terms of biting commentary and wit is "Wall Street Shuffle" from 10cc's *Sheet Music* album in the early '70s. They too were brilliant wordsmiths at that time.

As for the music, it kicks off with an acoustic intro before Scott's rock-solid, four-on-the-floor drums take over. Florian's guitar is right up front, and (almost) no one misses Martin Barre. In the turnaround section, Ian's voice becomes "discombobulated," much like on Tull's "Aqualung," which then leads into a spot-on flute solo followed by some super shredding from Florian. I can hardly keep up with him on air guitar!

I genuinely believe this track would have been a brilliant addition to any era of Jethro Tull or Ian Anderson's solo work, and it will certainly stand the test of time. It's one of my favourite Ian tracks from the four-and-a-bit albums I've reviewed so far.

Score 17/20

GERALD GOES HOMELESS

Swing It Far

In scenario two, Gerald's journey takes him from super-rich to super-poor. Whereas before, wheeler-dealer Gerald was in control as a banker, now he becomes a tragic victim spiralling out of control. This is a lyrically dense and grim song, filled with sorrow. Our hero — or rather anti-hero — is sexually abused at school, misunderstood by his parents, and ultimately ends up a damaged adult living on the streets near Camden Market. He may even be resorting to offering sexual favours for money to survive. Poor Gerald is cast adrift, bewildered from such a young age, perhaps ending up as a bearded tramp slumped on the pavement. Perhaps Ian Anderson was never "Aqualung"; it was just Gerald Bostock all along.

Musically, the track begins with a light, melodic touch,

featuring acoustic guitar and a delightful piano, accompanied by Ian's spoken words. The beautiful melody contrasts sharply with the harsh, raw lyrics. Ryan O'Donnell makes his singing debut on line seven, portraying the youthful, innocent Gerald. The track takes a surprising turn when, around 1:20, the chorus crashes in, with the full band playing heavy, intense rock. By the second verse, Ian and Ryan are singing in unison, and Ian then takes over solo, gently guiding the song to its conclusion with acoustic meanderings once more. Notably, there is no flute played in this track.

Score 13/20

Adrift And Dumbfounded

Gerald, now a homeless adult, can barely recall his childhood, his memories obscured by the alcoholic haze and insomnia he endures. Poor chap, he is now truly "adrift and dumbfounded," with nowhere to go and "no appointments to keep." The lyrics evoke a deep sense of longing for some good news and optimism!

Musically, this track is incredibly cool, with a bluesy, rootsy feel. The acoustic/electric contrast and pacing remind me of "Rocks On The Road" from Jethro Tull's *Catfish Rising*. Florian's guitar complements Ian's vocal lines perfectly. As with much of *TAAB 2*, the sound is enriched by the prominent use of Hammond organ, played by John, a nostalgic nod to *TAAB 1* and early Jethro Tull, when John Evan's Hammond was a key feature. Midway through, each instrument takes a turn to solo — guitar, flute, and piano — over a fast-paced rhythm. However, it's the slower sections that truly elevate the track. The absolute highlight, though, is Florian's final, sleazy bluesy lead guitar lick right at the end, which alone makes the song worth the price of admission.

Score 15/20

GERALD THE MILITARY MAN

Old School Song

In this scenario, Gerald graduates from the school officer cadet force to be commissioned in the real army, ready to fight for (then) Queen and country with valour, honour, and integrity. These deeds could well be the stuff of song and folk memory. "Old School Song" is lyrically gung-ho, glorious, and something to be treasured.

However, the backdrop to this song is rooted in the brutal reality of the wars in Iraq and Afghanistan, where the British were drawn into the "war on terror" alongside the Americans. In stark contrast to the idealised image of a heroic "fly-boy" helicopter pilot coming to save the day, the reality was often far less glorious. By the time British troops withdrew from both countries, over 600 service personnel had been killed in action. The truth is it was far from glorious.

"Old School Song" draws on a musical motif vaguely reminiscent of *TAAB 1* and presents a jaunty, lively, and optimistic tone. It evokes the attitude of "we'll sort the b******s out, come home in glory, and still be in time for tea." The track features plenty of instrumental flourishes, with a mid-paced rhythm and some nice flute playing. It's a good track, though not my personal favourite. But brace yourselves, because another epic is coming up — one of Ian's finest ever.

Score 11/20

Wootton Bassett Town

Royal Wootton Bassett is a small market town in Wiltshire, England, with a population of about 13,500. Between 2007 and 2011, the bodies of service men and women killed in action in Iraq and Afghanistan were repatriated to RAF Lyneham, just south of Wootton Bassett. The coffins, draped in Union Jacks, would then be carried through the town in procession on their way to the John Radcliffe Hospital in Oxford.

Initially, the Royal British Legion paid their respects, followed by the townspeople who gathered along the High

Street to watch the procession. These events were widely reported in the media, becoming a significant part of the national consciousness. In 2011, repatriations were moved to RAF Brize Norton.

At the time, Ian lived locally and had the opportunity to witness the processions firsthand. He was deeply moved by the experience and channelled his thoughts into the lyrics of what became an outstanding anti-war song. The powerful words convey the pain and terror of facing probable death in the desert, followed by the repatriation through Wootton Bassett. Ian pays tribute to those who stood in silent respect for the fallen, shedding "their tears for the military man." It's an emotional, poignant lyrical piece, and the music is not bad either, complementing the sentiment perfectly.

The song features a full band performance, with lead guitar and flute adding subtle embellishments over a powerful, pounding riff that's nothing short of head-banging brilliance. Ian's vocals are laden with sadness and melancholy, perfectly suited to the track's theme. His later vocal delicacy lends the song a sense of nobility, warmth, and empathy — ideal for the tribute it expresses. This track transcends the military man, Gerald Bostock's story, becoming something far more significant. It's a remarkable song, and surprisingly, the music reappears later in the album, with different lyrics.

Score 18/20

GERALD THE CHORISTER

Power And Spirit

Back to school, and this time Gerald, the young pupil, feels the calling of the Lord. He senses the power and spirit guiding him towards becoming a clerical man. For him, it is a Christian religious experience, though with just a hint of darkness creeping in. In the final verse, the devil seems to intrude, perhaps attempting to gain a foothold over Gerald — if I've interpreted the lyrics correctly. This is a classic Ian Anderson lyrical twist, ending on a slightly pessimistic note. Ian had been employing this kind of melancholic punchline for over forty years by 2012.

"Power and Spirit" begins with a delicate, quaint melody before the full metal band erupts in the "I sense" section. This musical theme is then repeated, with the final heavy section evoking the dark side. Alas, it seems that the story can only end in tears... or perhaps bankruptcy.

Score 13/20

Give Till It Hurts

This is my favourite acoustic interlude and track from *TAAB 2*. As a youngster, raised in a Catholic household, I distinctly remember the collection tray being passed around during Mass for donations. But what was it all for? I used to imagine that perhaps it cost money to turn the communion wine into the blood of Christ during the service — at least, that was my infantile delusion.

In this song, Gerald, now a chorister and vicar but touched by the Devil, thinks nothing of fleecing his debt-ridden congregation to stave off the threat of church bankruptcy — or perhaps to line his own pockets. Of course, it is the regular churchgoers who end up bankrupt. Hallelujah!

The highly entertaining lyrics fit perfectly with the jaunty, lively Celtic-inspired music, which Ian sings with gusto and enthusiasm. It's probably best to leave your wallet or purse at home while enjoying this great song.

Score 16/20

GERALD: A MOST ORDINARY MAN

Cosy Corner

There's nothing wrong with leading a cosy, normal life — working in the corner shop, "open all hours" (well, nine to six) — but perhaps only for a microcosm of a lifetime, not until death do us part. Otherwise, it could get terribly dull. This slightly mundane, brass-assisted song seems to reflect the everyday existence of Gerald. Pete Judge's additional instrumentation includes trumpet, flugelhorn, tenor horn, and E-flat tuba, and he certainly earns his session fee here.

As usual, Ian's lyrics are a showcase of his wordsmithing skills. He seems to be delving into the psyche of the ordinary Gerald, though the mention of Harold Pinter (whose plays often began with normal people revealing a darker side) and "slow Passion Play" suggests there's more to this scenario than meets the eye.

What sums up scenario five for me, though, is the reference to model railways — something I can relate to (I'm planning to convert my loft into model railway splendour "one day," or perhaps "never"). This also allows Ian to sneak in a reference to "Locomotive Breath." And by the way, does anyone know if you can still get Frey Brentos Pie in 2025? Answers on a postcard, please.

Musically, a shuffling Salvation Army brass band provides the backdrop for Ian's spoken lyrics as the song gently meanders towards its quick conclusion. I remember with much amusement watching John O'Hara in the live tours, pressing keys and gadgets on his keyboard to replicate the brass band, while Ian animatedly chatted over the top, and the rest of the band looked on, bemused!

Score 12/20

Shunt And Shuffle

It's time to return to some rock and out goes the brass. Ian repeats some of the lyrics, reinforcing the theme of normality in a more foot-tappable manner. The mention of Frey Bentos comes up again — twice, no less. Were they sponsoring the album?

The instrumental track features the full band, with fluttering flute and flashy guitar embellishments, and it flows along quite nicely. Next up, it's time for something completely different again.

Score 14/20

CONVERGENCE: DESTINY, FATE, KARMA, KISMET
A CHANGE OF HORSES
A Change Of Horses

This track doesn't quite fit with the overall flow of *TAAB 2*. It feels more like a stand-alone effort that was written long before Ian developed the *TAAB 2* concept. Both Dave Rees and Martin Webb, in the excellent *Tull* fanzine *A New Day* (Issue 103), had strong opinions on "A Change Of Horses," and I tend to agree with them.

Dave explains that the track was originally written for Anoushka Shankar (something I didn't know), intended as an Indian-sounding piece with sitar. Both Dave and Martin lament the use of John's accordion as a substitute for the sitar when the song was eventually woven into the *TAAB 2* narrative. They also struggle to understand how it fits with the overarching theme of the album.

Personally, I like the song, but it feels out of place on *TAAB 2* and perhaps a little too long. However, it's not all bad — I really enjoy Scott Hammond's understated, syncopated drumming on the track, which has a "jazz cool" vibe to it.

Now, let's look at the lyrics. The writer (Gerald, in his multi-scenario form) is either fifty years away from home or has had four hundred thousand hours pass in his life, which works out to forty-five years and eight months.

So, is Gerald fifty or forty-five-ish? There's a discrepancy of nearly five years in Gerald's timeline, according to Ian's arithmetic lyrics. Unless I'm missing something (or being a bit "thick as a slide rule"), this seems odd.

Regardless, "A Change Of Horses" marks a significant period of change and turning points in Gerald's five lives. The lyrics hint at a "new day" dawning, where "yesterday is an old day," suggesting a vaguely optimistic outlook for Gerald's future.

Apologies to the Jethro Tull song "A New Day Yesterday" for misappropriating its title to explain the lyrical direction. The lyrics are good, but they're perhaps not wordy enough to justify such a long track, and they don't advance Gerald's story much further. This song could have easily fit on any Ian

Anderson or Jethro Tull album — it's very good but stands more independently than within the *TAAB 2* narrative.

The music, though, is still enjoyable. Even without a sitar, it conveys a promise of Eastern and Indian influences. The track has a long intro (as befits an eight-minute song), lasting 1:40, before the gentle vocals come in. After that, there are cool, relaxed solos and noodling interludes that sound like classic prog Tull. While I like the track, it's clear that it's more of an outlier compared to the cohesive *TAAB 2* concept running through the other songs. I suspect it was added at a late stage in the album's production, when Ian felt the music — if not the song itself — was too good to leave out.

Score 11/20

22 MULBERRY WALK

Confessional

It's time for a five-verse update on the five different Gerald scenarios. Here, Gerald the banker goes bankrupt, Gerald the homeless man lands on his feet in a civilised civil partnership, while Gerald the chorister is cast out, with "not a prayer" after being "caught hand in till."

The lyrics are brilliantly crafted, providing a Gerald-ish catch-up that fits perfectly with the mood and sentiment of "Confessional." In the final two scenarios, Gerald the military man is invalided out of the army to assist his fellow service personnel, and Gerald, the most ordinary man, sells the shop and puts his model railway up for sale on eBay. Well, if I had known, I might have bought it — perhaps I could have helped Gerald out!

The first minute of the track is dominated by a harpsichord, before a more swollen organ and grungy guitar sound takes over the song. The final minute features an instrumental rock-out, complete with some great drumming from Scott around the kit. This is an okay track, but it serves mainly as the overture for another truly standout song on the album.

Score 11/20

Kismet In Surburbia

I'll lay my cards on the table: I absolutely love this track. It's undoubtedly up there with the best of Ian Anderson and Jethro Tull. Not only is the music exceptional, but the lyrics also successfully wrap up and conclude the five-story arc of Gerald.

Kismet is a Turkish word, derived from Arabic, meaning fate or destiny. The lyrics convey that it was very much Gerald's fate to be finalised in the five scenarios presented here. At least all the Geralds have somewhere to live, each at their own version of Mulberry Thoroughfare. They could all meet up at the Mulberry Community Centre in a parallel universe to compare their life stories. Once again, the storytelling is brilliant, a hallmark throughout *TAAB 2*.

The Banker seeks forgiveness, the Chorister acquiesces to fate (Kismet), and the Military Man remembers fallen comrades. Meanwhile, the Most Ordinary Man collects stamps indoors and watches steam trains outdoors. But the real gut punch comes from the Homeless Man, who now lives in relative luxury, only because his "slipped away" late partner bequeathed him these comforts. It's one of Ian Anderson's signature songs with a sad ending.

And then there's the magnificent music. The track opens with acoustic guitar, followed by chunky, thick electric guitar chords. The rhythm drives forward with guitar, flute, and organ interludes. The turn around at the "Mulberry" lyrics is just brilliant, leaving the listener wanting more. Ian's vocals, as throughout the album, are clear, with each word concise and precise.

There's a strange last thirty seconds — the "take away" section — where the track jolts and jerks aimlessly, disconnected from the main body of the song. It could be an eccentric lead-in to the final track, which isn't half bad either. However, this doesn't detract from the fact that "Kismet In Suburbia" is truly the bee's knees, or the dog's b******* of a song!

Score 17/20

WHAT-IFS, MAYBES, MIGHT-HAVE-BEENS

What-Ifs, Maybes, Might-Have-Beens

Why not take one of the best songs from *TAAB 2* (track 5), reword it slightly, and place it as track 17 to conclude the album? That's exactly what Ian Anderson did, and the result is a fitting conclusion to the *TAAB 2* journey. This decision brings the concept of endless possibilities and multiple universes full circle, inviting us to reflect on our own "what-if" moments — those pivotal pinch points where life could have turned out entirely differently. It's a magnificent way to end the album, tying its themes together beautifully.

Oh, and nearly forgot — right at the end, almost as an afterthought, there's a quaint little tune that starts with the line "So you ride yourselves over the fields..." It feels oddly familiar. Where have I heard it before? Can't quite place it... but it sounds great. Just "what if, maybe" Ian could get another album out of it?

Score 18/20

Thick As A Brick 2 reached No. 35 in the UK album charts and performed respectably on the Billboard charts, climbing to No. 55. It fared even better in Europe, peaking at No. 13 in Germany and No. 12 in Finland. Critical and fan consensus generally settled on 3 out of 5 stars or 7/10 ratings, acknowledging its quality while conceding that it didn't match the legendary status of *Thick As A Brick 1*.

Descriptions such as "sterile" and "overproduced" were levelled by some, but these are not terms I would use. I appreciate how everything is discernible, particularly Ian's more delicate, aged vocals, which add a certain melancholy that complements many of the tracks. For this, we have Steven Wilson — Porcupine Tree polymath and exceptional mixing engineer — to thank.

While the lyrics of *TAAB 1* were famously obtuse and esoteric, those of *TAAB 2* flow more straightforwardly, offering a coherent narrative. This made it far easier for lyrically challenged listeners like me to follow the story. The musicians on *TAAB 2* may not be the household names of Tull's golden era, but they deliver commendable performances, with Florian Opahle stepping in admirably as a Martin Barre substitute.

Many fans lamented the absence of long-time drummer Doane Perry following the 2011 split, but his replacement, Scott Hammond, provides understated yet skilful drumming. Dave Goodier on bass and John O'Hara on keyboards both play solidly, doing precisely what is needed.

However, *TAAB 1* remains an iconic prog-rock epic of the 1970s — and arguably all time. Following such a masterpiece was always going to be a monumental challenge for *TAAB 2*.

Should it have been a Jethro Tull album? Unlike *TAAB 1*, which is synonymous with Jethro Tull, *TAAB 2* emerged as an Ian Anderson solo album. Forty years later, the landscape had shifted. Could it really have been Jethro Tull in 2012 without Martin Barre? For me, it wouldn't have sounded right.

By 2025, the waters have settled, and *TAAB 2* fits more comfortably under the Jethro Tull banner. But in 2012, it was too soon after the acrimonious 2011 split to feel like an authentic Tull reunion. Besides, as an Ian Anderson solo album, it allowed me to explore it in depth for this book — which has been a lot of fun!

Does it work without Martin Barre? Surprisingly, yes. Florian Opahle is an exceptional guitarist, both in ensemble work and solos, and he has his moments to shine. That's not to say Martin wouldn't have done an outstanding job — of course he would have. In 2025, it's unfortunate that Martin still seems upset about the events of 2011, and while a reconciliation and performance together would be wonderful, it seems unlikely. My final word on the matter is that it's a shame Martin wasn't involved, and I would have preferred his presence. But Florian proved himself more than capable, showcasing his extraordinary talent.

The live tours that followed *TAAB 2* were widely considered a success, and I thoroughly enjoyed the performance I attended at the Ipswich Regent. The concert was split into two parts: *TAAB 1* was performed first, with Ian's vocals extensively supported by Ryan O'Donnell, whose exceptional singing allowed Ian to focus on playing more flute.

TAAB 2 followed in the second half, with Ian's mellow,

mature vocals perfectly suited to its tone. *TAAB 1* was far more demanding on Ian's 21st century vocals in the first half but *TAAB 2* was flawless, just going to show what a good singer Ian can still be with the right material. The ensemble playing was very good, and the show had a vibrant energy. The absence of a "'Lung/'Breath" encore divided opinion, but personally, I didn't mind — the double-dose of *Thick As A Brick* was more than enough to satisfy.

My views on *TAAB 2* align with much of the critical consensus. It's a very good album, but *TAAB 1* remains in a league of its own. My favourite tracks include the rockers "Banker Bets, Banker Wins," "Wootton Bassett Town/What-Ifs, Maybes, Might-Have-Beens," and "Kismet In Suburbia." I also have a soft spot for the lively "Give Till It Hurts." The overarching theme of Gerald's five scenarios and the return to a conceptual storytelling album is particularly appealing.

Ultimately, the album is a great success. Yet, in an alternative timeline, one tantalising thought lingers: perhaps this is the finest Jethro Tull album that never was. What if...? Maybe...

TAAB 2 (Thick As A Brick 2)

6
Homo Erraticus

Just when you thought it was safe to go back outside, it turns out the myth and legend of Gerald Bostock might be real after all. Ian Anderson insists so, claiming Gerald lives next door to him and had a major stake and say in shaping *Homo Erraticus*.

At this point, I'm starting to think Ian Anderson might actually be a figment of Gerald Bostock's imagination. Could it be Gerald who's been the lyrical and musical genius behind Jethro Tull all along? The evidence stacks up — Gerald even gets to write an article in the album's sleeve notes, for f**** sake!

So, what's the truth? Does Gerald Bostock actually exist? Ian has certainly outdone himself this time as a progtastic purveyor, crafting an album so richly layered with complex musical and lyrical ideas that *TAAB2* feels lightweight in comparison. To tackle this, I may need an IQ enhancement and copious amounts of caffeine enrichment. Despite the daunting concept — essentially Ian's attempt to condense the history of the world into just over fifty minutes — there's a playful whimsy that underpins *Homo Erraticus*. After all, Ian would have to be as mad as the soon-to-be-mentioned Ernest T. Parritt to let crazy Gerald write the lyrics. And yet, that's exactly what he did.

At this point, I can only conclude that everyone involved in making this album is entirely bonkers — and perhaps so are the fans and critics who listen to or write about it. Time for a lie-down...

Several days later, I now feel brave and enhanced enough to attempt a start of sorts, to delve into this album. I'm indebted to the extensive sleeve notes written by Ian and Gerald, which outline the convoluted background to this project. The sheer complexity of the concept can likely be blamed on Ian for allowing the patently insane Gerald to take part.

Here's the gist: There was once a man named Ernest T. Parritt, who served in the British Army in India during the 1800s. While stationed there, he either contracted malaria or fell off a horse (the precise details are lost to history), leading to bouts of acute insanity.

During one of these episodes, Parritt devised a strange book titled "Homo Erraticus" (The Wandering Man), which he wrote while residing in various sanatoriums for lunatics in the Swiss Alps. The sole surviving copy of this book eventually surfaced in Linwell Library, a suburb of St. Cleve, where it was discovered by none other than Gerald Bostock in 2013.

Gerald, who as a precocious child genius had collaborated with Ian on *Thick As A Brick* in 1972, now returned in his (im)mature middle age to write lyrics inspired by Parritt's book. Despite the fact that Gerald is plainly nuts and a socialist, Ian decided to compose music to accompany his words.

The is all explained in great erudite detail by Ian, in his and Gerald's nine pages of sleeve notes in the album booklet, where both men elaborate on what the "Homo Erraticus" book is all about. In brief, the book describes the past lives of Ernest T. Parritt, who imagines himself as a Neolithic hunter-gatherer, an Iron Age blacksmith, a Saxon invader, a Christian monk, a 17th-century grammar schoolboy, a turnpike innkeeper, a Brunel-era railway engineer, and Prince Albert, husband of Queen Victoria. (Is there no end to this man's delusions?) He even prophesies that in a future life, he will become both Ian Anderson and Gerald Bostock. It is all the inanely insanely the honest truth! Truly, you couldn't make this up — except they did.

But wait, there's more. After chronicling these past lives, Ernest ventures into future prophecies and revelations. His book spans a timeline from 7000 BCE to 2044 CE, with Gerald annotating the relevant historical periods for each song in the sleeve notes. These dates are included in the text at the start of every song analysis. Thus, in just fifteen tracks and fifty-one minutes, *Homo Erraticus* covers nearly 9,000 years of human history. Is it progtastic brilliance or pretentious overreach? Perhaps both.

While it's not essential to read the sleeve notes before listening to the album, doing so provides valuable context and enhances the enjoyment of this immensely ambitious concept. If you relish albums with labyrinthine narratives before you've even pressed play, this one is for you.

The line-up remains unchanged from *TAAB2*: Ian Anderson on vocals, acoustic guitar, and flute; Florian Opahle on electric guitar; John O'Hara on keyboards and accordion; David Goodier on bass; Scott Hammond on drums; and Ryan O'Donnell providing additional vocals.

By 2014, three years after "the split," the absence of Martin Barre is less keenly felt than on *TAAB 2*. However, as always, one wonders how much richer the album might have been with Martin's distinctive guitar work. That said, Florian Opahle once again proves himself a superb musician.

Steven Wilson was unavailable to mix the album, so Jakko Jakszyk (of King Crimson fame) stepped in for mixing and mastering duties, with Carl Glover at the Aleph Studio designing the cover. The mysterious masked figure on the cover — could it be Ian, Gerald, or perhaps, nature forbid even the mummified remains of Ernest T. Parritt? — adds an enigmatic touch.

The album was recorded in January 2014 and released on 14th April 2014, clocking in at just under fifty-two minutes. *Homo Erraticus* continues in the prog-rock conceptual vein of *TAAB2,* being an even more serious attempt to be the ultimate Ian Anderson "Jethro Tull like" album.

Was it any good? Did it meet expectations? Absolutely. I'll discuss chart positions, reviews, and the subsequent live concerts after an interval. But first, it's time for a song-by-song analysis. Off to refill my coffee cup — this one's going to require a fully caffeinated neural circuited brain!

Part One: Chronicles

Doggerland

This all takes place about 7000 BCE. In the heart of the North Sea, geographically and euphemistically described as "the middle," lies a shallow area of water about fifteen metres deep. This region, bounded by England, The Netherlands, and Denmark, has long been prized for its fishing. Over centuries, Dutch fishing boats known as Doggers frequented this productive area, giving it the name Dogger Bank.

However, Dogger Bank's significance extends far beyond its marine bounty. Seabed samples from the area have revealed astonishing evidence: fossils, pollen, mammoth tusks, and ultimately, signs of Mesolithic human habitation dating back several thousand years. This region was once Doggerland, a temperate rainforest ecosystem that offered its inhabitants everything they needed to thrive as hunter-gatherers. For about a million years, Doggerland connected the British Isles to northwest Europe, standing above sea level until it was submerged approximately 6,000 years ago — practically yesterday in geological terms.

During that time, the UK was not an island. One can't help but wonder how history might have unfolded differently had Doggerland remained above water. Perhaps there would have been no Brexit, no Channel Tunnel, and certainly no "Doggerland" as the opening track on *Homo Erraticus*. In such an alternate timeline, Ian Anderson might have penned a song about the European Parliament instead!

Now for Ian's — no, correction, Gerald's — lyrics, which, as always, are a challenge to decipher. The song seems to trace an evolution from ancient Albion (a term derived from Greek and later used by the Romans) to the modern "England." Gerald's vision transitions from the Doggerland of "boar and elkes and wolves" to a contemporary scene involving holidaying pensioners and "little Englanders." Or at least, that's what it seems to suggest. To be honest, Gerald, your clever wordplay is a bit elusive here.

In my first book on Jethro Tull, I often struggled to keep up with Ian Anderson's literary brilliance. With Gerald Bostock now in the mix, he seems to be even more obtuse, it appears little has changed. He is Ian Anderson on steroids!

Musically, "Doggerland" opens with an instrumental section led by guitar and flute before giving way to a heavier, metallic chorus underscored by crunchy electric guitar. Florian Opahle takes centre stage with a blistering shredding guitar solo halfway through, showcasing his impressive technique. The production is crisp and clear, bringing Ian's warm and gentle latter-day vocals to the forefront.

The track has drawn comparisons to "Roots To Branches," both in style and spirit. Dave Rees, writing in *A New Day Magazine* (Issue 112), highlights the similarity, and I agree — there's a definite link, which is no bad thing.

"Doggerland" is a strong opening to *Homo Erraticus*, blending historical narrative, thought-provoking lyrics, and engaging instrumentation. Its combination of ancient themes and modern sensibilities sets the tone for the monstrously ambitious journey that lies ahead.

Score 14/20

Heavy Metals

This takes place from 750 BCE to 43CE. Scientifically, the term "heavy metals" encompasses a broad range of dense metallic elements, including the toxic Mercury and Arsenic. Even iron, which serves as the base for steel — so prominently referenced in Gerald Bostock's lyrics — fits this category. Gerald, ever fond of wordplay, appears to revel in the double entendre of the song's title, linking the scientific concept of heavy metals with the musical genre known for its loud, distorted, and rebellious "sex 'n' drugs 'n' rock 'n' roll" guitar riffs. Yet, the song opens deceptively softly, resembling a quaint acoustic ditty about a blacksmith forging iron.

However, as is often the case with Ian Anderson and Gerald Bostock's lyrical collaborations, things are not as straightforward as they first appear. From iron comes steel, a material integral to the manufacture of guns and other instruments of war. Ian, who has previously expressed an interest in collecting firearms, likely contributed his knowledge of historical gun manufacturers, a detail woven into the second stanza of the song.

Oh dear, by the third stanza, the narrative takes a darker turn, name-dropping Harry S. Truman and Robert Oppenheimer, who invented the atomic bomb and it is all the fault of heavy metal! Here, heavy metals such as Uranium and Plutonium reach their most destructive form, becoming the very core of nuclear weaponry. What begins as a quaint ode to ironworking escalates into a grim meditation on humanity's capacity for destruction. A quintessentially Andersonian twist, where even the most cheerful tunes mask sobering themes.

Musically, the song features a charmingly cute, sing-song melody, with Ian's vocals dancing over chordal changes. The contrast between this light-hearted composition and the weighty subject matter is striking. Despite its brevity — clocking in at just one minute and thirty seconds — the track encapsulates the bleak inevitability of a world shaped by heavy metals and their devastating potential.

The themes explored here resonate again in "Mrs Tibbets" from Jethro Tull's *The Zealot Gene*, where Ian revisits the atomic bomb's haunting legacy. Clearly, this is a subject that continues to inspire his music and storytelling.

Score 10/20

Enter The Uninvited

This takes place over the period from 43 CE to 1960. One of the greatest lyrical achievements in music has to be Billy Joel's "We Didn't Start The Fire." In this iconic track, Joel lists historical and cultural events spanning from 1949 — the year of his birth — through to 1989, the year the song was released. Although I haven't personally counted them, there are said to be 119 separate references packed into just over four minutes. It's the ultimate "list song."

Here, Gerald Bostock and Ian Anderson attempt something similar with their own unique twist. The lyrics chart the history of immigration into the UK, including not just people (such as the Romans) but also artefacts (like nylon stockings) and cultural imports (for instance, *Star Trek*). The first two verses focus on historical "invasions" by the Romans and then the Angles, Saxons, Danes, and Normans (with "Willy Conker" being a playful reference to William the Conqueror).

From there, the song shifts to listing more modern cultural influences, primarily from the United States. While not quite matching Billy Joel's tally, there are twenty-eight references in total, ranging from "Elvis hips" to *The Sopranos*, all squeezed into just over four minutes. How does Gerald, the ever-brilliant madcap lyricist, manage it?

Musically, the track opens with ghostly, atmospheric sounds before transitioning into a jaunty, strutting processional rhythm, where everybody and everything pops in for a spot of whimsical immigration. Flute and guitar take the lead in a tight, unison performance, giving the song a strutting, sprightly energy. The melody carries a playful optimism, complementing the theme of integration and cultural exchange. Ian delivers the list-heavy lyrics with precision, almost rapping them in places, and his warm delivery injects the song with charm.

While it may not quite rival Billy Joel's classic in terms of impact or complexity, this is an enjoyable track that brims with cleverness and wit. It's a lively interlude in the album, paving the way for what comes next — a true standout moment.

Score 11/20

Puer Ferox Adventus

This takes place over the time period 313 CE to 600 CE. On most Jethro Tull or Ian Anderson albums, there's often one song that stands out as a true classic — a track that exudes ambition and grandeur. These pieces tend to be longer (this one clocks in at over seven minutes) and often feel "mini-symphonic" in structure, with intricate, sometimes over-the-top lyrics and a dynamic musical composition full of acoustic "light" and powerful "shade." Think of Tull epics like "Budapest" from *Crest Of A Knave* or "Black Sunday" from *A*. On *Homo Erraticus*, that song is undoubtedly "Puer Ferox Adventus." Let's face it — if you're going to title a rock song in heavy-duty Latin, then let's face it, it better live up to the hype.

The title, "Puer Ferox Adventus," translates to "Wild Boy Coming," which is arguably the easiest part of Gerald Bostock's lyrics to grasp. The rest is layered with historical and religious references that require some effort — and perhaps a history textbook — to unpack. The song begins with Ian, adopting a godlike tone, referencing Lindisfarne, the Northumbrian island famous for its early Christian monastery. In the second verse, "Meet in Milan" likely alludes to the Edict of Milan in 313 AD, which allowed Christianity to flourish in the Roman Empire. By the final verse, "Via Dolorosa" references the path in Jerusalem associated with Jesus's journey to crucifixion.

The overarching theme appears to chart the rise of Christianity, but questions remain: Who is the wild boy coming? Who is the angry man? The "new age dawning" described in the lyrics doesn't sound particularly optimistic. Perhaps this track serves as a thematic companion to "Mine Is The Mountain" from Jethro Tull's *The Zealot Gene*, where the figure of the high altitude God is similarly stern and vengeful. Gerald's fascination with religion — and perhaps Ian's own — resurfaces here, as it has in past Tull classics like "My God" from *Aqualung*. I do wonder if madcap Gerald was religiously repressed as a child as both he and Ian always have something to say on these high faluting matters.

As always, I can't claim to fully grasp the lyrics, and "Puer Ferox Adventus" is no exception. The use of Latin adds a dramatic flourish, though some might find it a touch over the top. While Ian Anderson is likely to be remembered more for his revolutionary flute playing than his Latin titles, this track certainly has its own unique charm.

Now for the music — and what a special piece of music it is! The track opens with a thunderous drone, setting a solemn tone, as Ian, the monk delivers his vocals with a severe gravitas. A captivating melody follows, with organ and guitar interjections creating a call-and-response dynamic. Ian now as God sings with conviction, embodying his on high narration. By the third verse, the rhythm shifts into a more frenetic pace, driving the song toward a thrilling climax.

The instrumental section, which begins around the four-minute mark, is a highlight. Guitar and flute interplay elevate the track both tonally and emotionally, while Scott Hammond's drumming is outstanding, adding urgency and depth. The song circles back to a final verse before building to an instrumental crescendo, closing the track with majestic intensity.

Despite its lyrical complexity — perhaps overly so for some (*Thick As A Brick* vibes, anyone?) — this is a magnificent piece of music. "Puer Ferox Adventus" stands out as a cornerstone of *Homo Erraticus*, balancing high-concept ambition with musical brilliance. It's a testament to Ian Anderson's ability to craft epic, thought-provoking compositions even after decades in the game.

Score 16/20

Meliora Sequamer

This takes place during the 12th century. For my sins — or perhaps because of them — I attended a Roman Catholic boys' grammar school, where Latin was part of the curriculum. I never fully understood why we had to learn it, though I was fascinated to discover that everyday terms like *exit* (way out), *status quo* (as it is), and even *TARDIS* (late or slow), from Dr Who derive from Latin. We also studied Ancient Greek, which I found far more enjoyable. Words like *logic* and *politics* come from Greek, and we had the added novelty of a different alphabet — alpha, beta, gamma, and so on. I wonder if Gerald might consider a comeback album in Ancient Greek for Ian to sing. Now, that would be something else!

I went to grammar school in the twentieth century, a few years after the "song pupil" in "Meliora Sequamer," who seems to have been at school from the twelfth century onwards. Strangely enough, as late as 1967, when I started school, the teachers still wore gowns and mortarboard hats. Corporal punishment was also alive and well — I once received the cane across my hand for climbing onto the school roof to retrieve our break-time football. We had inkwells, Latin lessons, and the extinct language even featured in the Catholic Mass. These lyrics resonate with me deeply. Gerald, did you write this song about me? It certainly feels that way. I think you did. Thank you for helping me to exorcise some of my school-year demons. Catholic grammar schools were still intimidating places in the 1960s and 1970s.

Unlike "Puer Ferox Adventus," I love and easily follow the lyrics in "Meliora Sequamer." Gerald even kindly provides a translation for the title: "Let Us Follow Better Things." That being said, the music here doesn't quite reach the same heights as "Puer Ferox Adventus."

The song begins with a church-like quality, as Ian's vocals follow the chordal progression. He seems to be joined by Ryan O'Donnell on the "O Domine" line, with Ryan taking the lead on a few lines here and there. The instrumental interlude, featuring Florian's lead guitar, is functional rather than extraordinary, and then it returns to Ian's meandering vocals. The melody feels somewhat dour and "see-sawish" in its rhythm. While the tune may not stand out, the strength of the lyrics makes the song worthwhile.

This track is a quintessential *Homo Erraticus* piece — where the brilliance of the words outshines the music.

Score 15/20

The Turnpike Inn

This takes place in and around 1750. A turnpike was historically a gate that blocked a road until a toll was paid. While the term has largely fallen out of use, toll roads still exist in the UK today — for instance, part of the M6 around Birmingham. However, no one refers to the toll barriers there as "turnpikes," the word having become somewhat antiquated. In earlier times, as turnpikes slowed journeys, it was natural for inns to spring up at these pinch points, offering weary travellers sustenance, ale, and even a change of horses.

Gerald's lyrics recount a journey through the turnpikes, fraught with the dangers of highwaymen, who would mercilessly rob travellers at gunpoint. He references John Austin, the last man to be hanged at the Tyburn Tree gallows in London in 1783. Although Austin himself was not a highwayman, many highwaymen met a similar fate at the gallows in earlier years. Naturally, any travellers lucky enough to survive such perils — and still possess a few coins — might have sought solace at a Turnpike Inn to "drown their sorrows."

Musically, the track features a riff-driven arrangement with pounding drums and additional vocals by Ryan. It's a mid-paced rocker, characteristic of Ian Anderson and Jethro Tull's style. However, once again, the lyrics are the standout feature, offering more intrigue and depth than the rather plain, monochrome tune.

Score 10/20

The Engineer

This takes place in 1847 a few years after Box Hill railway tunnel was complete. Genesis — the band, not the biblical epoch— recorded a brilliant track called "Driving The Last Spike" on their *We Can't Dance* album, which paid tribute to the navvies who risked life and limb to build Britain's railways. There's a thematic link between that song and Ian Anderson's "The Engineer" from *Homo Erraticus*.

Navvies get a mention in the first verse here, specifically those who worked on the construction of Box Tunnel on the Great Western Railway (GWR). It's worth noting that thirty-six navvies tragically lost their lives in accidents during the tunnel's construction — grim evidence of a time when "health and safety" and yellow hard hats were unheard of in those bygone days.

The GWR itself was overseen by the visionary engineer Isambard Kingdom Brunel, who championed a unique broad-gauge track system with a width of 7 feet ¼ inch. His reasoning was that broader tracks would allow for faster speeds and greater passenger comfort with wider locomotives and carriages. However, while Brunel engineered the GWR between London Paddington and Bristol to this specification, the standard gauge of 4 feet 8½ inches — developed "oop north" — ultimately became the global norm. By the late 1800s, the GWR's broad gauge had been phased out. Nevertheless, Brunel's route to

Bristol, along with its magnificent infrastructure — including Box Tunnel — remains in use to this day, a testament to his enduring engineering genius.

Gerald Bostock really goes to town, delving into historical storytelling with the lyrics to this track. One can only imagine how many hours of research went into crafting this detailed narrative. Brunel himself even gets his own song — a tribute he surely would have appreciated if he'd lived another 156 years. He passed away in 1859, but his legacy lives on through both the railway and, now, this track.

Does the music live up to the lyrical ambition? It begins with John O'Hara on the accordion, lending a distinctive texture, followed by delicate, tinkling piano work. The rest of the band joins in for a full ensemble performance, complemented by Ian's trademark "breathy" flute playing. As a tune, it feels more engaging and dynamic than "The Turnpike Inn," striking a fine balance between musicality and narrative depth.

Score 14/20

The Pax Britanica

This takes place from 1815 to 1914. This is a wordy song, with forty-one lines of lyrics packed into just over three minutes, all about Queen Victoria, Country and the British Empire. The period of Pax Britannica represents a time of relative peace between the world's superpowers, with Britain at the forefront, seemingly ruling much of the globe through its empire and acting as the world's policeman. Those were/weren't the days.

Gerald's torrent of ambitious lyrics reflects this imperial status. He touches on themes of trade, commerce, and the paternalistic "civilising" of British colonies. Architecture, cricket, and a strict moral code were all part of the cultural legacy handed down to the colonies during the reign of Victoria and Albert.

Once again, Gerald attempts to convey complex ideas through his intricate lyrics. He references the "Hansa", a medieval group of German traders, and the "Enfield Pattern Gun" as symbols of Britain's military strength. The "Saxon

Prince" is mentioned as well — he was a son of a sovereign of the Kingdom of Saxony — but it's unclear why he's included. Is Gerald being a bit too clever for his own good here? It almost feels as though Ian has given Gerald complete creative freedom with the lyrics, and if Ian were solely responsible, they might have been more tempered. In any case, this one has been a bit of a struggle, and I'm off for an early bath.

As for the music, it begins with a guitar riff followed by a jaunty piano, all underpinned by fluttering flute. The tone of the music is far too cheerful for a song about the rise of a (possibly tyrannical) empire. If the subjugated peoples had written this piece, it would likely sound very different. However, the upbeat melody perfectly captures the illusion of the halcyon days of a peaceful empire, at least for the British, when all seemed well with the world. But history was about to change — and not for the better. That said, all is not lost, as Ian Anderson is about to deliver three high-class tracks that will lift our spirits.

Score 11/20

Part Two: Prophecies

Tripudium Ad Bellum

This takes place between 1914 to1939. This is an instrumental track, primarily in 5/4 time. If you decide to dance to it, make sure to add an extra wiggle on every fifth beat — otherwise, you might risk tripping over! Gerald had the night off, so there are no lyrics to either confuse or amuse me. However, as a parting gesture, GB left us with a title... in Latin! *Tripudium* refers to a religious dance performed in triple time by the Romans, while *Ad Bellum* translates to "right to war." In a 2014 interview in *A New Day* magazine, Ian referred to it as a "forerunner of line dancing."

This lively instrumental piece represents the idea of "dancing off to war" in 1939, seemingly carefree. Perhaps Gerald could have titled it *Ambulatio* (Latin for "walking"), as in "walking off to war," but that wouldn't have been nearly as fun. "Dancing off to war" sounds much more ironic and fitting, if you're aiming for a deeper, prog-rock touch. And if you want to be even more *progtastic* and profound, a Latin title is just the way to go — well done, Mr GB!

Once past the thudding repeated riff at the start, I really enjoy the music in this track. The main melody, rhythm, and overall feel remind me of "Living In The Past," the early Jethro Tull single. The riff returns at the end, leading into a cacophonous organ solo, no doubt symbolising the tumult of war. This is definitely one of my favourite tracks on the album.

Score 16/20

After These Wars

This all happens around 1950. I really enjoy this one, and hooray — I think I finally understand most of GB's lyrics! It's an optimistic song. By 1950, Britain was well on its way to recovering from World War II. Food rationing was gradually coming to an end, except for meat, which continued until 1953. Television was becoming a regular part of daily life, penicillin was curing infections and "raising the dead," and combine harvesters were "keeping us fed." All seemed well with the world, and there was fun to be had. Gerald's upbeat, optimistic lyrics capture this spirit perfectly.

The music features a great melody with a stately, medium-paced rhythm, supported by piano and guitar accompaniments. And just wait for the guitar solo towards the end, where Florian goes full metal shredding. I think this is his best solo from all his work with Ian on *TAAB 2* and *Homo Erraticus*. Ian waits until the end to add a touch of fluttering flute, rounding off the track beautifully.

Score 16/20

New Blood, Old Veins

We move on 10 years to 1960. This is just a fantastic tune. While I've been somewhat indifferent to some of the musical tracks so far, this one stands out as brilliant for me — it's definitely my favourite on the album!

Gerald does a decent job with the lyrics, which reflect the rise of package holidays. My first family holiday in a car was in a

Morris Traveller, which gets a mention in verse 2. However, we were heading to Scarborough from Nottingham, not off to paint the continent red, as Gerald did with his friends, crossing the Channel by ferry. Gerald's lyrics are peppered with place names, showing he's well-travelled, but my favourite line is "melanoma is such a pain," which feels particularly relevant in this age of ultraviolet exposure and global warming.

The music is a stunning blend with a jazzy swing and syncopated feel, just rocking along with great vocals and flute from Ian. Unfortunately, it's all over in just two minutes and thirty-two seconds. After playing it recently, after so many years, as Kylie Minogue would say, "I just can't get it (the tune) out of my head!" Ryan joins in with additional vocals, and I love the jingling piano at the end. The lyrics and music are in perfect harmony here. This could be a contender for my favourite Ian Anderson solo song!

Score 18/20

Part Three: Revelations

In For A Pound

It is 2013 and it is a "Cheap Day Return" interlude for Ian and Gerald, filled with female dalliances, barley beer, and the ability to indulge without spending much. But enjoy it while it lasts, because things are about to get tough in the next song. "Here we go!"

This is a light, singsong ditty where Ian, as is typical for this album, follows the chords. It's all wrapped up in just one minute and thirty-four seconds.

Score 10/20

The Browning Of The Green

Now more or less up to date in 2014 onwards, Gerald addresses exponential population growth and the pressures it places on greenfield sites for new housing and infrastructure. Gerald draws inspiration from the lyrics of "Locomotive Breath" where

Ian similarly explored the rapid growth of the population. Both songs suggest a lack of foresight and, perhaps, contraception. As Gerald puts it in the current song, "Six or seven (children) might be nice."

The musical track is frenetic and riff-driven, with a sound reminiscent of other songs on the album, where the full band plays a flurry of notes with flute and guitar riffing in unison. Once again, the lyrics are arguably more engaging than the music.

Score 11/20

Per Errationes Ad Astra

With great foresight and insight back in 2014, Gerald has written some lyrics for Ian that bring us up to date, 10 years later in 2024, and it's heavy-duty stuff. "Per Errationes Ad Astra" translates to "to wander through the stars," perhaps signalling the next stage in the evolution of Homo Erraticus. The problem, however, is that it may be too late for some cosmic wonder — oh dear. A reckoning awaits in the "Cold Dead" of the next song!

Ian delivers his lines with a bit of echo, interspersed with occasional singing and spaceship sound effects. The overall tone feels quite grim. As part of an ongoing suite of songs, it works well, though a typical short acoustic interlude sung by Ian would have been a better choice otherwise.

Score 9/20

A Cold Dead Reckoning

This one is to be set in 2044. It's the end of the world as we know it, unless we can find the new Eden Ian sings about in the final verse — and we have just nineteen years to find it, as I write this in 2025. Good luck with that. There's a nice bit of symmetry here with "Looking For Eden" and now, in 2014, he's still searching, with Gerald's lyrical help. It could make for a good book title.

The song starts off slow and cold, but I really like the riff. It's simple but effective, foot-tappable and almost sing-along friendly. After a pleasant flute interlude around the four-minute mark, the riff softens, giving way to a piano-led section, which is particularly effective. I do wish Ian had left more of that in. A clap of thunder follows, and then a sweet Celtic melody leads the fade-out, leaving just a hint that after all these years of searching since 1983, Eden might be just around the corner.

Score 17/20

Homo Erraticus is a brilliantly flawed yet fascinating album. It reached No. 14 on the UK Album Chart and No. 13 on the German Album Chart, though it largely faded elsewhere. By 2014, I'm sure Ian was starting to realise that the album might have sold better had it been released under the Jethro Tull moniker. It was generally well received by fans and critics, with many considering it superior to *TAAB 2*. A typical rating from reviewers would likely be around 3.5 stars out of 5. If you enjoy concept albums that are complex, conceptual, and replete with Latin titles, as well as a wealth of historical detail all written by an insanely ambitious lyricist — then this album is definitely for you.

Personally, I feel that by allowing "The Gerald" character to write the lyrics, enabled Ian to produce his most complex and expansive historical writing yet, all be it underpinned with a hint of surreal humour. We can thank Gerald and his mentor Ernest T Parritt for that While I generally enjoyed the lyrics, a great deal of research was required to understand the people and places referenced in the songs. As for the Latin titles, I'm not entirely sure about them; they do seem a little pretentious at times. We can definitely lay the blame for that at Gerald's door. After all, Ian did aim to create the mother of an ultimate concept album, one to rival *Passion Play*, but with a discernible epic story telling narrative. The use of whimsical humour, which brought back Ernest and allowed Gerald Bostock to flourish as a wordsmith, gave *Homo Erraticus* an edge over the more obscure serious and confusing *Passion Play*, at least lyrically. Musically, however, *Passion Play* still outshines *Homo Erraticus* in terms of pure tunes and arrangements, in my view.

The Ian Anderson Band really get their chance to shine, particularly Florian Ophale, whose shredding virtuosity nearly makes us forget Martin Barre. Florian's role here was far less controversial than on *TAAB 2*, where many fans were disappointed by Martin's absence. Scott Hammond, despite attracting some negative comments, is an understated and underrated drummer who quietly excels. John O'Hara earns praise from all IA and JT fans, as he plays the accordion throughout the album. David Goodier, meanwhile, does what's needed, taking root and establishes himself as an underrated bass player.

The *Homo Erraticus* tour, which I saw in Ipswich, was great fun. Like with *TAAB 2*, the album was played in full during the first half, followed by a set of JT "hits" after the interval. It must have been a good show because my previously sceptical wife, Linda, really enjoyed the concert and even added "Aqualung" and "Locomotive Breath" to her playlist without telling me.

There were some hints that concert venues weren't full during the UK tour, but that wasn't the case at the gig we attended. It's also refreshing to see that Ian and the 2025 version of Jethro Tull, which includes three members from the 2014 band, are still selling out venues eleven years later. In fact, I've never seen a half-empty gig for Ian Anderson or Jethro Tull. Some reports suggested that audiences were only showing up for the greatest hits section, but if that was true, they missed a treat! Ian and the band were exceptional, with Ryan adding mime and extra vocals so Ian could focus more on flute. The whole crowd, from the fans to the ice cream vendors at the theatre, left the show happy.

As I noted in my song-by-song analysis, I feel the lyrics often outshine the music on parts of the album, where many tracks sound somewhat similar with a "routine" rock feel. My favourite track was "New Blood, Old Veins," an absolute powerhouse that "swings and rolls" as much as it rocks. I can't get the tune out of my head after revisiting it. I'm also fond of "Per Ferox Adventus" for its epic instrumental climaxes, and "Cold Dead Reckoning" for its grungy riff and the hint of "finding Eden" optimism at the album's conclusion.

"Tripudium Ad Bellum" is another favourite for its quirky rhythm — it could easily be the perfect "drunk at the disco" track. My favourite lyrics, though they might be a challenge for non-train spotters, come from "The Engineer," as I'm a bit of a secret train buff myself and knew all about track gauges, the Great Western Railway, and Isambard Kingdom Brunel. In fact, I probably could have written the lyrics to that one — if not the music.

I'll be comparing the albums in more detail in a later chapter, but suffice it to say that *TAAB 2* and *Homo Erraticus* are very similar as prog rock epics. But which will come out on top?

As for the overall winner across all six albums, you might have an inkling if you've followed my individual song scores. It's time to reveal which one has triumphed.

Conclusion

If you need a reminder, each individual song was given a score out of 20 in the text of each album. While I didn't comment on these scores at the time, I will do so now in the conclusion. I have since calculated the average score for each album by dividing the total score by the number of tracks, which gives us the overall mark out of twenty for each album. The precise tally of the scores has been independently verified by my mathematically meticulous wife, and the results are now confirmed. The wait is over!

In order, we have:

1) *Divinities: Twelve Dances With God*
   Av Score and final mark = 14.1

2) *Rupi's Dance*
   Av Score and final mark = 13.6

3) *TAAB2*
   Av Score and final mark = 13.4

4) *The Secret Language Of Birds*
   Av Score and final mark = 13.3

5) *Homo Erraticus*
   Av Score and final mark = 13.2

6) *Walk Into Light*
   Av Score and final mark = 12.9

It was a close race throughout, except for the gap between first and second place. There is a clear winner, and I must admit, I'm surprised. Until now, I wasn't sure which album would come out on top — how could an album with no lyrics or vocals possibly beat the others? But it did!

With *Divinities*, it's clear that I enjoy the tunes, appreciate the backstories of their composition, and buy into the unifying concept of the album. Aside from two tracks, it doesn't have any massive standout gems, but it maintains a consistent high score across the board, with only a couple of tracks that might be considered vaguely weak.

If there's one thing that has remained constant over nearly sixty years of recording, it's Ian's remarkable ability to find a good melody. That combination of varying pitch and changing rhythm is consistently outstanding for me and makes for great music that particularly appeals to my ears.

This is even more evident on *Divinities*, where the absence of lyrics is more than compensated for by some of Ian's most incredible melodic creations. Where does he find them? Perhaps plucked from everywhere and nowhere. A special mention must also go to Andrew Giddings, who brings Ian's sublime tunes to life with his exceptional arrangements.

The two acoustic albums, *Rupi's Dance* and *The Secret Language Of Birds*, are very similar, with *Rupi* just edging it. Both albums have consistent scores, but only two standout tracks, one on each album. They represent typical Tull "lite" acoustic tracks that Ian has sprinkled throughout Tull albums over the years. Once again, we have his great melodies, interesting, mostly accessible lyrics, all well-arranged.

Both of these later, conceptually-driven Tull albums score similarly. Overall, *TAAB 2* has the best musical tracks, while *Homo Erraticus* stands out for its challenging "history of the world" lyrics. Both albums, especially *TAAB 2*, feature some truly magnificent songs, although other parts of the albums score a little lower. They are modern updates on *Thick As A Brick 1* and *Passion Play*, with less nebulous and obtuse storytelling but still complex enough prog lyrics to satisfy the nerdy concept album enthusiast.

I wasn't surprised that *Walk Into Light* ended up at the bottom of the list, which is a shame, as Ian's songwriting — particularly in terms of melody and chord sequences, though not always the lyrics — was approaching its peak.

Unfortunately, the album's anaemic, mechanised electronica soundscape, without a drummer, has not aged well. There's no way these songs would ever be recorded the same way by Ian in the future. Perhaps if artists like Ed Sheeran or Adele took on some of these tracks as covers with an updated soundscape, they might go down a treat. Maybe I'm overhyping it a bit here, though?

Across all the solo albums, there are eighty-two songs, and while I can't possibly rank them all from worst to best (unless the money was upped a lot, and even then I might need a decade or two), I could certainly do a top 10. Go on then, let's see what makes the cut!

1) In The Grip Of Stronger Stuff
   (Divinities: Twelve Dances With God)
2) Wootton Bassett Town/What-Ifs, Maybes And Might-Have-Beens
   (TAAB2)
3) Looking For Eden
   (Walk Into Light)
4) Banker Bets, Banker Wins
   (TAAB2)
5) New Blood, Old Veins
   (Homo Erraticus)
6) In Times Of India (Bombay Valentine)
   (Divinities: Twelve Dances With God)
7) Kismet In Surburbia
   (TAAB2)
8) Cold Dead Reckoning
   (Homo Erraticus)
9) A Raft Of Penguins
   (Rupi's Dance)
10) The Habernero Reel
    (The Secret Language Of Birds)

Let's consider these in reverse order. "The Habanero Reel," the only track from *The Secret Language Of Birds*, is fun, light, dancy, and spicy. I've really enjoyed seeing this track performed live by either Ian Anderson or Jethro Tull over the years. It was a close call between "The Reel" and "Sanctuary" from *The Secret Language Of Birds* for the coveted No. 10 spot.

"A Raft Of Penguins" soars and flutters into the stratosphere (hyperbole, or what!), and gets my vote for No. 9 for mentioning "The Whistler" in the lyrics. I could have also chosen "Not Ralitsa Vassileva" from *Rupi's Dance* for this spot.

"Cold Dead Reckoning" deserves an honourable mention at No. 8. It is the last Ian Anderson track on his final solo album and brings us full circle by referencing "Eden" in the lyrics, which ties in with the title of this book.

"Kismet In Suburbia", the first of three outstanding rock tracks from *TAAB 2,* pushes ahead with musical turnarounds at every Mulberry location mentioned, making it something of a classic at No. 7.

At No. 6 is "In Times Of India (Bombay Valentine)," which incorporates classical, jazz, and even rock 'n' roll overtones to produce a great final track on *Divinities.*

"New Blood, New Veins" from *Homo Erraticus* zooms in at No. 5 for its fantastic lyrics and quirky, swinging melodic rhythm. This may be a surprise entry for some.

"Banker Bets, Banker Wins", the second hit from *TAAB 2* in our top 10, takes No. 4. It's another great rock song that could easily fit on any seventies or eighties Jethro Tull album.

The title track of this book, "Looking For Eden" from *Walk Into Light*, takes No. 3. It has the best melody and tune of all eighty-two songs. It's just missing a flesh-and-blood drummer. The deep, meaningful, and yearning lyrics only add to its allure. I would have loved this song to be No. 1 to align with the book's title, but the songs in the top two wouldn't have worked as titles. No. 2 is too long, and No. 1 could have implied that Ian Anderson was an alcoholic or drug addict during the making of the six albums.

At No. 2 is "Wootton Bassett Town/What-Ifs, Maybe, Might-Have-Beens." I've combined these two tracks, as they share (more or less) the same tune, but with two different sets of great lyrics. If you think I'm cheating a little, you might be right, but getting two songs for the price of one can't be bad.

Musically, it's absolutely epic, with all the best of Ian Anderson's and Jethro Tull's rock splendour. The double dose of lyrics for the same music is a great touch. "Wootton Bassett Town" is Ian's heartfelt tribute to those who have fallen in battle, while "What-Ifs, Maybes, Might-Have-Beens" revisits the overarching theme of alternative scenarios for Gerald Bostock, echoing the spoken words from track 3, "Might-Have-Beens."

At the end of "What-Ifs", there's a nice lyrical touch about "riding yourself over the fields" that I still can't place — though I'm sure it'll come to me, if only I weren't still thick as a brick!

So, that leaves us with No. 1 — it better be good, and by golly, it certainly is! "In The Grip Of Stronger Stuff" earns its place not just because it's a magnificent classical Celtic fluting extravaganza, but because every time I've seen it performed live, either by Ian or Jethro Tull, it has been absolutely outstanding!

Don't believe me? Ask the audience. Having attended many Ian Anderson or Tull concerts over the years, I've never witnessed a reaction to any other song or track like this. It seems to receive a standing ovation every time it's played live, with one of those wonderfully euphoric moments at its final note when even Ian Anderson cracks a wide grin. It's a stunning piece of music, and in my subjectively biased view, it's the absolute best of all eighty-two Ian Anderson tracks reviewed in this book.

Of the other seventy-two tracks not mentioned in the top 10, most are still really good. Ian is nothing if not consistent when it comes to songwriting, with only the odd misstep. I'm not going to name the tracks that I consider weaker — you can check my scoring for that — but I will say that I'm not a fan of the spoken word segments. Right, that's enough of that.

Of course, the fun element in this conclusion is when you, the reader, may disagree with my choice of best album or best song. And that's completely fair! You'll have your own opinions, but I'm sure that, somewhere along the way, there will be some broad agreement between us fans, the critics, and perhaps even Ian himself about what's truly great and what's not so great. Overall, in my hopelessly biased but slightly discerning view, the eighty-two tracks represent a fantastic body of work.

However, Ian was not entirely alone, even if he was technically 'solo.' It's time to pay tribute to some of the supporting cast.

Andy Giddings joined Tull as the brilliant keyboard wizard in the early nineties, becoming Ian's main collaborator on the sophisticated, classically-influenced *Divinities* album, after which he formally adopted the name Andrew.

He also became Ian's main collaborator on the acoustic *The Secret Language Of Birds*. It's a great credit to Andrew that he was able to make such significant contributions to these contrasting albums. He was still involved in 2003, contributing to *Rupi's Dance*. Should he have had writing credits on *Divinities* and *The Secret Language Of Birds*? Only he and Ian know.

Peter-John Vettese, who earned several writing credits as Ian's collaborator on *Walk Into Light*, can certainly take some of the blame from fans who weren't fond of the album's electronica approach. However, Peter's skill and contributions undeniably enhance several great tracks, such as "Looking For Eden."

On the later two concept prog-rock albums, *TAAB 2* and *Homo Erraticus*, the core Ian Anderson band — Florian Ophale, John O'Hara, David Goodier, and Scott Hammond — did Ian proud. Each member was allowed to shine, particularly Florian. Other musicians, mainly Ian's German friends, including Leslie Mandoki and The Sturcz Quartet (referenced in the *Rupi's Dance* chapter), also made significant contributions.

So how do these solo albums compare to those of Jethro Tull? In the 1980s, *Broadsword And The Beast* was considered one of the best JT albums, alongside *Crest Of A Knave* (which, in my opinion, was equally impressive). While *Walk Into Light* doesn't quite match these two, it does share some similarities with JT's *Under Wraps* from 1984. Both albums lacked a drummer and adopted a distinct 1980s electronic, synth-driven sound. Both also featured some great melodic songs, albeit with somewhat mismatched arrangements. Perhaps the edge goes to *Under Wraps* over *Walk Into Light*, primarily because of the "Tull lite" acoustic version of the title song to become "Under Wraps 2," which stands out as a highlight.

By common consensus, the 'real' Jethro Tull sound was most evident on *Roots To Branches* in the 1990s. The album included a mix of acoustic sections, rock moments, and a considerable amount of bamboo and wooden flute playing, contributing to an Eastern vibe that also appeared in Ian's flute work on *Divinities*.

Conclusion

Although *Divinities* could never truly be a Tull album, it serves as a superb musical cousin and a 'warm-up' for *Roots To Branches* (released in May 1995, with *Roots* following in September of the same year). The melodies on both albums are exceptional.

The Secret Language Of Birds and *Rupi's Dance* feature acoustic songs that could have comfortably appeared on any Tull album. With typical acoustic guitar, flute, and accordion arrangements, these tracks compare favourably to some of the best acoustic Tull material.

This brings us to the two "Jethro Tull" Ian Anderson albums. The obvious comparison for *TAAB 2* is *TAAB 1*. I would rate *TAAB 1* at 18/20 for side one of the vinyl and 16/20 for side two, averaging 17/20 — higher than *TAAB 2*, which scores 13.4/20. However, the original *Thick As A Brick* is widely recognised as one of the best prog rock albums of all time, while *TAAB 2* begins to hold its own, particularly with its three stand out rock tracks.

For *Homo Erraticus*, the natural comparison is with *Passion Play*, which might score 15/20 — still better than *Homo Erraticus* at 13.2/20. However, the historical storytelling lyrics in *Homo Erraticus* give it an edge over *Passion Play*, where the obtuse, surreal lyrics are more difficult to follow. That said, the music of *Passion Play* is, for me, more entertaining than some of the more "samey" tracks on *Homo Erraticus*, even though Ian himself no longer holds *Passion Play* in particularly high regard. Both of these albums stand up well against more recent JT releases like *The Zealot Gene* (2022), *RökFlöte* (2023) and *Curious Ruminant* (2025), with some fans perhaps even preferring them.

Most of the eighty-two solo tracks, with some rearrangement, could easily fit on any Jethro Tull album. They may have been overlooked, neglected, or underrated simply because they weren't part of a Jethro Tull release.

Now, the next big question: would these albums have sold more under the Jethro Tull name? The answer is undoubtedly yes, for four out of the six albums. *Walk Into Light*, with its electronic sound, and *Divinities*, with its classical influence, could never have been Tull albums in a million years, but the other four could have, especially the latter two concept prog albums.

The most glaring underperformer among the solo albums would be *TAAB 2*, which seemed to beg for a follow-up as a Jethro Tull album. *Homo Erraticus* was also very much in the classic Tull style and might have enjoyed enhanced sales under the Jethro Tull name.

By 2017, Ian had come to a similar conclusion about future sales, which led him to write *The Zealot Gene* and eventually release it as a Jethro Tull album.

While there are many books on Jethro Tull, there seems to be a distinct lack of literature dedicated specifically to Ian Anderson's solo albums. However, a 96 page booklet is available as part of a vinyl box set of Ian's six solo albums released, called "Ian Anderson 8314 Boxed" This was put out on the 23rd August 2024, as I was coming to the end of writing the main body of this book. They are 20 sides of 10 discs and you may have to remortgage your house to pay lots of money for it — £200 plus! It consists of all the albums and some additional live tracks. I have not got it yet, as like many people of my age the record player has mysteriously disappeared into the attic with out end, many years ago!

Until now, references to his solo albums have mostly appeared as appendices or brief mentions in Tull books and magazines, and that's about it. So, if you're a Tull fan discovering Ian's solo work for the first time through this book, I sincerely hope you've enjoyed it, learned a little more, and are now listening with an open mind to some great music that you might be hearing for the first time. The individual CDs or streaming might of course be an easier and cheaper way to listen or re-listen, rather than buying the vinyl box set. If you are reading this as a newcomer or just a "returner" after so many years since you last listened, then give the solo albums of Ian Anderson a spin. You won't be disappointed!

So, what of Ian Anderson? Is there anything new to say? Let's try this: he won't be remembered for allegedly inventing "rubbing elbows" or for the dubious claim of having invented the claghorn — the mysterious wind instrument heard on "Dharma For One" from Tull's *This Was* (1968), which sounds like a vacuum cleaner. He might not be remembered as an all-time great rock singer either. As an acoustic guitar player, perhaps Roy Harper did it just a little better.

That leaves us with Ian's phenomenal flute playing, which, in my view, remains unparalleled. Whether in folk, classical, or jazz styles, Ian absolutely nailed it. No one does it better. And as a songwriter, Ian has been, is, and will continue to be outstanding, with his beautiful melodies and profoundly meaningful, entertaining lyrics that make us think, smile, and feel.

But Mr Anderson, please — no more solo albums before this book goes to press!

And with that, I conclude this book. I'm off to begin my next project: *The Rise, Fall, And Rise Of Gerald Bostock: His Role in the Evolution of Ian Anderson and Jethro Tull in 200 Pages of Purposeful Pretentious Prose*. It's bound to be a bestseller!

And that's that. Thanks, Ian! Bye for now.

Acknowledgements

I would like to thank my Jethro Tull and Ian Anderson "expert by default" wife, Linda, who continues to have to put up with my endless meanderings on all things Tull. She did her usual fabulous job initially proof reading, while continuing to explain to "thick as two short planks" me that sub clauses in sentences need commas!

My thanks also to Jerry Bloom at Wymer Publishing, who has given me this fabulous opportunity to put out my second book. I am particularly grateful to Laura Shenton for her constructive proof reading and editing.

And finally, of course I have to thank Ian Anderson for putting out six marvellous solo albums that are very much worth writing about.

Oh, and very remiss of me. I should be thanking Gerald Bostock for everything else, without whom etc…

Bibliography

There is a limited amount of information available in books specifically about Ian Anderson's solo albums, but references can be found in various works on Jethro Tull, including:

On Track... Jethro Tull: Every Album Every Song by Jordan Blum, which includes a brief chapter at the end discussing Ian Anderson's solo albums.

The Pocket Essential Jethro Tull by Raymond Benson, which also features a short chapter at the end covering the first three solo albums, up to *The Secret Language Of Birds*.

I also referred to my own earlier work, *Life Is A Long Song: A Compendium of Jethro Tull in 33 1/3rd Songs*. Hopefully, I managed to avoid repeating myself!

Additionally, *Record Collector Presents Jethro Tull* (September 2023) provided useful background information on the solo albums.

The best source of information, by far, was the excellent Jethro Tull fanzine *A New Day*, edited and written by Dave Rees and Martin Webb. With the exception of *Walk Into Light* (which pre-dated the fanzine), the publication offered a wealth of reviews, live gig reports, and interviews with key figures, including Ian himself, covering the latter five solo albums.

I was also greatly indebted to the insightful sleeve notes that Ian has provided for most of the albums. These notes were not only informative but also highly entertaining, often worth reading in their own right. A book of sleeve notes, perhaps, Ian?

As expected, I consulted numerous Tull-related websites and, when necessary, may have referenced Wikipedia when no one was looking.

When all else failed, I had to rely on my own encyclopaedic knowledge of Jethro Tull and Ian Anderson (I really should get out more).

About The Author

Richard Taylor continues to be domiciled in Essex with wife, Linda and has no cats, dogs or goldfish. Pride of place in the Jethro Tull room currently goes to one slightly warped vinyl album with a frayed round the edged cover sleeve, plus 5 CDS of Ian Anderson's solo albums

This is Richard's third book after *The Good, The Bad And The Ugly: The Story Of 45 Mixed Up No 1 Songs* and *Life Is A long Song: A Compendium Of Jethro Tull In 33 1/3 Songs*.

There is speculation there are more authorly products in the pipeline.